This book focuses on the main issues of trade
and development and on the attainment of the
major development goals generally espoused in
the international community. These include rapid
development in the third world, sustained economic expansion in the industrial countries, and
the eradication of deep inequalities and of extreme poverty. A prerequisite for this is full participation in international and local societies, for
which the fulfillment of basic needs, introduced
and defined in the Bariloche model, is in turn
necessary.

Although these goals are highly normative, the
analysis in *The Evolving International Economy*
is descriptive, focusing on the particulars of market behavior, at both the domestic and international levels. It traces the ways in which markets
respond to policies, in the belief that policies
cannot be viewed in a vacuum but must be confronted with the responses of the market. International markets are one of the most powerful
forces governing the evolution of the work economy and must be taken into consideration when
analyzing alternative policies. The interplay of
domestic policies and international markets is
one of the main features of the authors' analysis.

The Evolving International Economy consists
of four parts. The first three give an overall analysis of the world economy, with commentary
and conclusions on major issues of trade and development. The fourth part provides, within the
context of the formal models, the intuitive basis
for the main results; rigorous proofs are found in
the references given to the technical literature.

GRACIELA CHICHILNISKY is a Professor of Economics at Columbia University as well as Senior Economist for the Banco Central de Argentina and Project Director for the United Nations Institute of Training and Research. Her writings include *Catastrophe or New Society?* (IDRC, 1976) and over fifty journal articles on economics and mathematics.

GEOFFREY HEAL is a Professor of Economics at the Columbia University Graduate School of Business. He served as Managing Editor of the Review of Economic Studies from 1969 to 1974. In addition to *The Theory of Economic Planning* (North Holland, 1973) and *Economic Theory and Exhaustible Resources* (with Dasgupta: Cambridge, 1979), he has written over fifty journal articles.

The evolving international economy

The evolving international economy

GRACIELA CHICHILNISKY
Columbia University

GEOFFREY HEAL
Columbia University

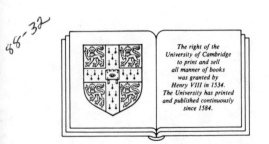

The right of the
University of Cambridge
to print and sell
all manner of books
was granted by
Henry VIII in 1534.
The University has printed
and published continuously
since 1584.

CAMBRIDGE UNIVERSITY PRESS

Cambridge
London   New York   New Rochelle
Melbourne   Sydney

Published by the Press Syndicate of the University of Cambridge
The Pitt Building, Trumpington Street, Cambridge CB2 1RP
32 East 57th Street, New York, NY 10022, USA
10 Stamford Road, Oakleigh, Melbourne 3166, Australia

First published 1986

Printed in the United States of America

Library of Congress Cataloging-in-Publication Data
Chichilnisky, Graciela.
The evolving international economy.
Includes index.
1. International economic relations.   I. Heal, G. M.
II. Title.
HF1411.C4159   1986   337   86-6124

British Library Cataloging-in-Publication Data
Chichilnisky, Graciela
The evolving international economy.
1. International economic relations
I. Title   II. Heal, G. M.
337   HF1411

ISBN 0 521 26716 1 hard covers

Contents

Preface   vii

 1 Introduction   1

Part I   Industrial economies and the international market   7
   2 Domestic policy issues   9
   3 Protectionism and the management of trade   23

Part II The role of developing countries   37
   4 Export strategies   39
   5 Armaments and North–South trade   65
   6 Aid, trade, and debt   73
   7 Resources and North–South trade   88

Part III Summary   103
   8 The evolving world economy   105

Part IV Theoretical background   111
   9 Adjustment, stability, and returns to scale   113
  10 Large-scale technologies and patterns of trade   122
  11 North–South trade and export policies   136
  12 Aid and transfers   150

Preface

The first version of this book was produced in partial fulfillment of a contract between the United Nations Conference on Trade and Development (UNCTAD) and the United Nations Institute of Training and Research (UNITAR), under which the latter undertook to assist the Secretary General of UNCTAD in the preparation of material relevant to UNCTAD VI, the sixth major international conference of the UN system on trade and development. It draws on results of economic studies, both theoretical and empirical, conducted by the authors over a number of years. Chichilnisky's studies originated in the production of the Bariloche model at Fundación Bariloche, Argentina, 1972–6, and were subsequently conducted under the auspices of the UNITAR Project on the Future at Harvard University, Columbia University, and the University of Essex with support from the U.S. National Science Foundation, the Rockefeller Foundation, the Institute for Mathematics and Its Applications at the University of Minnesota, and the Center for the Social Sciences, Columbia University. Their conclusions are embodied in Part II of this book. Heal's research was begun at the University of Sussex, and subsequently continued at the University of Essex, at Yale University, and at the Columbia Business School with support from UNITAR, the National Science Foundation,[1] the U.K. Economic and Social Research Council, the Institute for Mathematics and Its Applications at the University of Minnesota, the Center for Social Sciences, Columbia University, and the Faculty Research Fund of the Columbia Business School. His research was concerned mainly with the issues in Part I of the book.

The book focuses on the main issues of trade and development, and on the attainment of the major development goals generally espoused by the international community. These include rapid development in the third world, sustained economic expansion in the industrial countries, and the eradication of deep inequalities and of extreme poverty. A prerequisite for this is full participation in international and local societies, for which the fulfillment of basic needs, introduced and defined in the Bariloche model, is in turn necessary.

[1] The authors wish to acknowledge support from NSF grants SES-84-20244 and SES-84-09857.

vii

Although these goals are highly normative, our analysis is descriptive. It is focused on the particulars of market behavior, both at the domestic and at the international levels. It traces the ways in which markets respond to policies, in the belief that policies cannot be viewed in a vacuum, but must be confronted with the responses of the market. International markets are one of the most powerful forces governing the evolution of the world economy and must be taken into consideration when analyzing alternative policies. The interplay of domestic policies and international markets is a main feature of our analysis.

The book comprises four parts. The first three give an overall analysis of the world economy, with commentary and conclusions on major issues of trade and development. They make no use of either formal analysis or mathematical modeling. The intention here is to explain and illustrate rather than to provide rigorous proofs.

The fourth part of the book goes somewhat further than the first three in formalizing and making rigorous the earlier claims. It does not aim at the standards of formalization that one would ideally expect from professional journals. It attempts to indicate, for the benefit of readers with an acquaintance with basic economic theory, the nature of the models and the arguments that substantiate the discussion in the first three parts. It provides, within the context of the formal models, the intuitive basis for the main results. Rigorous proofs are found in the references given to the technical literature.

Our work has benefited from comments by many of our colleagues and a complete acknowledgment seems beyond our reach. However, we mention in particular Philippe de Seynes, Director of the Project on the Future at UNITAR, as well as the many comments and suggestions from Kenneth Arrow, Dragoslav Avramovic, Havelock Brewster, Joan Butler, John Cuddy, Gamani Corea, Juan de Castro, Avinash Dixit, Reinaldo Figueredo, Jerry Holtham, Ronald Jones, Soichi Kojima, John Llewelwyn, A. McIntyre, Darryl McLeod, Jan Pronk, Michael Sakbani, and Joseph Stiglitz.

Research assistance from Michael de Mello, Arlene Roberts, and Rachel Pohl is gratefully acknowledged. Maxine Braiterman and her colleagues in the word processing unit at the Columbia Business School provided invaluable help in the protracted task of preparing this manuscript. Finally we would like to acknowledge the editorial advice of Colin Day of the Cambridge University Press.

The opinions expressed here are entirely those of the authors, and do not reflect the positions of any supporting organization.

G. Ch.   G. M. H.

CHAPTER 1

Introduction

1.1 Background

The past ten years have witnessed major changes in the positions of industrial and developing countries in the world economy. Over this period, the developing countries have grown more, and have invested a relatively larger part of their GNP, than have the industrial countries. Developing countries have also increased significantly their role as export markets for the OECD countries, with their share of OECD exports being currently 40% of the total. They have in addition greatly increased trade among themselves. Many factors contributed to these developments, including resource pricing policies and a decline in the competitive position of industrial countries in certain markets. This decline has occurred both in heavy industries such as steel, and also in skill-intensive manufactures such as electronics. The reverse side of this coin is that many developing countries have increased their dependence on food imports from industrial countries.

Financial markets mirror the developments in goods markets. The current strains in the international monetary system reflect the lag with which our institutions adjust to a changing world economy. An example is provided by the genesis of the current debt crisis. Oil surpluses contributed to the growth of developing country borrowing during the past decade. At the end of the 1970s, high interest rates emerged in the United States and the United Kingdom partly as a policy response to concerns about inflation in an era of higher oil prices. Because of the increased interdependence in the world economy, these higher interest rates have had far-reaching international consequences. Their threefold increase in the four years to 1980 raised significantly the costs of servicing the borrowings of developing countries, and added impetus to the international debt crisis. A combination of high interest rates and a high exchange rate for the U.S. dollar has exerted financial pressure on those developing countries that incurred variable-rate, dollar-denominated loans.

Ironically, the debt problems of developing countries are leading to greater reforms of the international financial system than have been produced by many years of negotiations. The possibility of nonrepayment of major loans threatens the stability of some important international banks. The IMF has responded to this by proposing an increase in its quotas by 47%, a dramatic departure from its previous record. The Inter-American Development Bank also recently voted to increase its lending by one-third. Moving along similar lines, the U.S. banking community has lately allowed a moratorium of principal payments and a reduction in interest payments on the Mexican debt. International debt crises are of course not new[1]: What seems to distinguish the current one is the magnitudes involved.

In addition to gaining leverage over the international financial system, the developing countries have also gained in influence and importance because of their growing role in world trade. As already mentioned, they now provide a market for 40% of the OECD's exports. The community of interests between industrial and developing countries has therefore increased sharply. A natural consequence of this would be a revision of the policies of the IMF to take into account these strengthened international linkages. This includes, in particular, the impact that deflationary policies in developing countries have on OECD export markets.[2]

In a rapidly evolving economic environment, it is inevitable that our analytical tools require revising and adapting. Rather than succumbing to the appeal of familiar but dated concepts, one must move ahead toward a more realistic conceptualization of the problems and a more practical approach to their solutions. This book proposes economic tools for analyzing changes in the world economy. The relationship between domestic and international factors, and their impact on the evolution of the international economy, are its subject matter.

1.2   The main topics: a summary

There is a set of issues that have emerged during the past decade and that are central to an understanding of the international economy. A characteristic of these topics is that they link international and domestic policy areas in so integral a way that neither can be analyzed in isolation. The issues are as follows:

1. The recurrence of recession, the persistence and severity of unemployment in many industrial countries, and the emergence of protectionism.
2. The emergence in industrial countries of new technologies that lead to structural changes in domestic and international markets,

---

[1] See, for example, Chapters 7-9 of Arthur Lewis, *The Evolution of the International Economic Order,* Princeton University Press, 1977.
[2] For a more detailed discussion see John Williamson, *IMF Conditionality* and *The Lending Policies of the IMF,* Institute for International Economics, Washington, D.C.

and that challenge existing institutional arrangements and trading patterns.

3. The changing international environment facing the developing countries, and in particular the issues of international debt, of export strategies and of North–South trade in armaments.

4. The pricing of exhaustible resources, including oil, as a major issue in North–South trade, and in the international financial system.

5. The perceived limitations of the existing international financial institutions and the impact of declining transfers of wealth from industrial to developing countries.

Several factors underlie the rise of protectionism in industrial countries. One is the persistence of unemployment, in the aftermath of two severe recessions: Unemployment has been associated historically with demands for protection. Yet another factor in the rising tide of protectionism is the changing structure of international trade. The emergence of newly industrialized countries in world trade has led to intense competition in fields central to the industrial economies. Examples are the automobile and steel industries. In the industrial countries these industries have traditionally been important sources of employment, and also of demand for the outputs of other industries.

The pressures for protectionism also represent a failure to adjust to changes in the international economic environment. To the extent that it delays much-needed adjustments in industrial structure, protectionism may harm the industrial countries at least as much as it harms the exporting countries. However, an across-the-board liberalization of trade would be neither a likely event nor necessarily a desirable one, even if rapid structural adjustments were possible in the industrial countries. In our evolving world economy, trade policy must be more selective and integrated. This is a point that has certainly been appreciated by some of the most successful and export-oriented newly industrialized countries.

The emergence of new technologies in industrial countries has increased the importance of economies of scale in production. These new technologies may be very rewarding and contribute to higher living standards. However, they change the behavior of markets in a way that makes existing institutions inappropriate. With economies of scale, market price adjustments may not lead to equilibrium and to economic efficiency. International trade may fail to balance without sector-specific policies on the part of the trading partners. There may be no gains from trade on the part of developing countries that export labor-intensive products in exchange for industrial goods. Scale economies may also reduce the stability of the economy and make it more vulnerable to external shocks or to changes in other international market conditions. In such cases, new institutional arrangements are required to diffuse the gains from trade and to ensure smooth responses to evolving economic conditions.

The current international environment generates concern about the viability of export concentration on the part of developing countries, especially when based on the exports of traditional raw materials or labor-intensive commodities. International organizations have nevertheless emphasized export-led policies in recent years, frequently in response to balance-of-payments deficits in developing countries, but also as an over-all recommendation for rapid development. This originated partly from the apparent success of particular developing countries that pursued vig-orous export-led strategies in the early 1970s.

The economic basis for export-led strategies arises from particular views of economic development and of the international division of labor, views that rely on external "engines of growth" for developing countries. These views are questioned at present, and alternatives are being sug-gested. Export strategies require careful consideration of domestic condi-tions. Successful strategies must be accompanied by an increase in do-mestic productivity. In addition, correlations have been found between commodity export earnings and armaments imports of developing coun-tries; these also raise doubts about export-led strategies.

We shall analyze the possibilities and the limitations of export-led policies. A general endorsement cannot be given to one of the obvious alternatives, import substitution. Import substitution is too general, as it affects most sectors, and is at the same time too restrictive, as it affects only the supply side of the market. More selective strategies are needed. We analyze the extent to which engines of growth for the developing countries can be provided by domestic markets or by trade among the developing countries themselves.

Following a long period of inexpensive energy, the emergence of energy constraints and of higher oil prices in industrial countries has highlighted the importance of trade in extractive resources. For the past decade, oil pricing policies have been a major concern of industrial and of developing countries. Because of uneven patterns of consumption and of endow-ments, trade in exhaustible resources has emerged as a central issue in North–South trade.

The pricing of extractive resources has traditionally been a source of North–South conflict, with the exporting South arguing for better prices and the North resisting the South. Changes in the price of oil, however, have forged a strong interdependence between the North and the South, both in real and in financial markets. There is now a common interest between importers and exporters in keeping oil prices within a reasonable range – not too high, but not too low. Theoretical as well as empirical analysis argues for cooperative pricing policies in extractive resources.

We examine the impact of resource prices on the economies of the importing and the exporting regions. Recent experience of the impact of oil exports on economies such as Mexico, Venezuela, Ecuador, and Nigeria runs counter to conventional wisdom. These and other oil-exporting countries have benefited far less from oil exports than was expected. Similarly, extended periods of low oil prices have been a mixed blessing for importing countries. The evidence from the past decade contains important lessons on the effects of resource exports and their prices.

North–South transfers have been discussed for many years in the international development community. They emerged as the policy of choice in the reduction of North–South wealth differentials. The evidence shows, however, a consistent downward trend in such transfers. Currently they do not meet even half the minimum target proposed by the United Nations in the 1970s.

In the aftermath of the most recent recession in the industrial countries, the issue of North–South transfers has lost immediacy: In most industrial countries aid is no longer a policy priority. We analyze the impact of North–South aid and the conditions under which it is likely to reduce wealth disparities. International transfers are analyzed in the context of international markets. We analyze market responses, which play a large role in determining the final welfare effects of transfers.

Developing countries have on average sustained higher growth rates and savings rates than industrial countries in the past decade. Investment in developing countries has been financed in part by foreign capital flows. Many loans to developing countries originated in OPEC surpluses, which were recycled by Western banks. Short-term commercial debts accumulated rapidly over the past decade. The recent rise in interest rates in the United States and the United Kingdom, and the associated decline in the export markets of developing countries, has greatly increased the burden of this debt since the turn of the decade. Widespread concern exists about the sustainability of the current situation, and this has led to changes in international finance, as well as expectations of further changes in our international financial institutions.

Technological change and unemployment, the effects of exports of raw materials and of labor intensive commodities, the price of oil and the upheavals in the world's financial system – all are part of a gigantic puzzle. The following chapters should offer the reader some clues about how this might be assembled.

1.3   The structure of the book

The next seven chapters are concerned with analyzing the main issues and deriving conclusions. We begin with an overview of the economic situation of the industrial market economies, as a basis for the analysis of the international economy. We emphasize the relationship between macroeconomic problems and modern industrial structures in the industrial countries. The following chapters are concerned with the growth of protectionism and the emergence of managed trade, and with the main issues in the developing countries: an evaluation of export strategies; armament trade; the role of aid; international lending and international financial institutions; and the issue of international trade in exhaustible resources. Each section contains both an economic analysis and an indication of the policy implications of the analysis. The overall conclusions are drawn together in Part III, where they are also illustrated by reference to particular examples.

Part IV of the book then returns in more technical detail to four of the issues analyzed in the first two parts, and presents in outline the formal models upon which the earlier analysis and conclusions were based. The intention is to provide the reader acquainted with economic theory with an indication of how one proves the main results used in the text. Formal proofs are to be found in the references cited. The results that we select for this treatment are those sharing two characteristics: They are central to our analysis and are generally not well known, except perhaps in technically oriented professional circles. It may be several years before they find their way into textbooks, so it seems useful to make them more widely available here.

PART I

Industrial economies and the international market

CHAPTER 2

Domestic policy issues

2.1 Introduction

There has been a marked decline in the macroeconomic performance of the industrial countries since the early 1970s. This has taken the form of lower growth rates of GNP and of productivity, and of higher levels of inflation and unemployment. During this decade the industrial countries experienced the worst recession since the 1930s, and at the time of writing not all of them have recovered fully from this experience. In many Western European countries unemployment figures are in double digits, and inflation rates are high by historical standards.

There has been an extensive debate about the causes of this poor performance and about the policy measures necessary to remedy it. As yet there is little general agreement on these issues. An explanation that initially was widely canvassed attributed the recession of the 1970s to the increases in oil prices in 1973 and 1978–9. However, there is now general agreement that, although these price increases had some negative consequences for the industrial economies, these consequences were certainly not of the order of magnitude required to explain the recession of the 1970s. The principal causes must be sought elsewhere. We discuss the macroeconomic impact of higher oil prices in Chapter 7.

In this chapter we develop an alternative analysis of the macroeconomic characteristics and performance of advanced industrial economies. A central aspect of this analysis is the emergence of new technologies, which have fundamentally altered the macroeconomic characteristics of certain sectors of industrial economies. New technologies hold great potential for increases in productivity and living standards; however, like many previous technological advances, they require changes in social and economic organization and management if they are to be harnessed effectively. For example, the increased scale of production and the more extensive division of labor associated with the industrial revolution held great potential for increases in living standards; however, these were only realized fully after the development of new institutions as diverse as limited-liability joint stock companies and legislation on children's working conditions.

2.2   Macroeconomic performance and new technologies

Adam Smith observed that greater division of labor leads to higher productivity. He also observed that the scope for division of labor depends upon the extent of the market, so that it is more efficient to serve large markets than small ones. This point is central to the concept of economies of scale. "Economies of scale" and "increasing returns to scale" are phrases used to describe economic activities whose efficiency is greater at larger scales of production.

The emergence of new technologies in industrial countries has increased the importance of economies of scale in production. Examples can be found in electronics, telecommunication, transportation, and in many financial activities. In fact, any activity making extensive use of information or of telecommunication activities as an input will be characterized by economies of scale.[1]

It is also true that improvements in information technology have removed many of the managerial diseconomies of scale associated with communication and control in large organizations. It is precisely this type of diseconomy that was traditionally offered as a cause of diminishing returns at large scales of activity. Removal of these managerial diseconomies therefore postpones the incidence of decreasing returns to scale and makes increasing returns more likely.

Now, it has been recognized for a very considerable time that economies of scale are a major source of productivity growth. It is, however, generally acknowledged that they have become pervasive only in the postwar period.[2] The expansion of markets during this period, both through economic growth and through increased international trade, was able to sustain new technologies more effectively when these were oriented to large-scale production. This economic expansion thus provided

[1] There is an extensive empirical literature on the extent of economies in a range of manufacturing industries. For example: J. S. McGee, "Economies of Size in Auto Body Manufacture," *The Journal of Law and Economics* 16 (October 1973), 239–73; J. Ayler, "Plant Size and Efficiency in the Steel Industry: An International Comparison," University of Salford, Salford, 1981; C. Pratten and R. M. Dean, *Economies of Large-Scale Production in British Industry: An Introductory Survey*, Cambridge University Department of Applied Economics, Occasional Paper no. 3, Cambridge University Press, 1965; Z. Grilliches, and V. Ringstad, *Economies of Scale and the Form of the Production Function*, Contributions to Economic Analysis, North-Holland Publishing Co., Amsterdam, 1971. The role of information in generating economies of large-scale operation was first noted in R. Wilson, "Informational Economies of Scale," *Bell Journal of Economics* 6(1)(Spring 1975), 184–95.

[2] See, for example, the references cited in Elizabeth Bailey and Anne Friedlander, "Market Structure and Multiproduct Industries," *Journal of Economic Literature*, 20(3) (September 1982), 1024–48. An earlier study emphasizing the growing importance of increasing returns is N. Kaldor, *The Causes of the Slow Rate of Growth of the U.K. Economy*, Cambridge University Press, 1967.

an incentive for large-scale technologies, which then evolved rapidly. This evolution led to significant macroeconomic changes, which are the subject of this chapter.

We shall argue that scale economies have costs as well as benefits: They make the economy more vulnerable to shocks and reduce its ability to adjust to a changing environment.[3] As a matter of fact, an economy with increasing returns behaves very differently from one with diminishing returns and thus requires institutional arrangements and policies that are quite different.

2.3   Stagflation and economies of scale

Scale economies lead to outcomes strikingly different from those predicted by the textbook assumption of diminishing returns to scale. For example, a recession is commonly associated with lower prices, and an expansion with higher prices. With economies of scale these relationships are reversed. The explanation is simple.

In a recession demand and output drop. With diminishing returns, by definition, efficiency increases, so that costs and prices drop as well. This is the "leaner and fitter" view of the benefits of recession. Lower output leads here to more efficiency and to lower prices.

With increasing returns to scale this logic is reversed. Lower output levels lead to less rather than more efficiency, and thus lead to higher rather than lower costs and prices. Therefore with economies of scale a recession leads to inefficiency and to higher prices. This is usually called "stagflation," a phenomenon acknowledged to be difficult to explain in terms of the traditional assumption of diminishing returns.

Economies of scale therefore provide an explanation of stagflation that is not yielded by traditional assumptions. In stagflation we have recession

---

[3] At this point it is important to distinguish between an economy's vulnerability to shocks and the actual degree of cyclical variation that it exhibits. The phrase "increased vulnerability to shocks" means that, other things (including policy responses) being equal, a given shock has a larger impact. Now, there is empirical evidence to suggest that the degree of cyclical variation in the major macroeconomic aggregates of the U.S. economy has fallen over time (see J. B. Delong and L. H. Summers, "The Changing Cyclical Variability of Economic Activity in the United States," National Bureau of Economic Research, March 1984). This empirical evidence is not inconsistent with the argument that the economy is more vulnerable to shocks in the above sense because, over the period studied by Delong and Summers, macroeconomic stabilization policies improved greatly and automatic stabilizers such as unemployment and social security payments became much more widespread. Such institutional and policy reforms could have more than compensated for an increased responsiveness of the underlying economic system to shocks. Indeed, there is some evidence of such an increased underlying responsiveness: Delong and Summers refer to evidence "that the persistence of output shocks actually increased between the pre- and post-war periods."

accompanied by inflation, a recent phenomenon in several advanced industrial economies. Our arguments indicate that such malaise cannot easily be cured by further recessionary policies, for these could lead to further inefficiency and price increases.

The other side of this coin is expansion without inflation, which is the opposite of stagflation. With diminishing returns we are also at a loss to explain this current U.S. phenomenon, because the higher output should in principle lead to less efficiency and to higher costs. However, economies of scale can explain this easily: As the expansion proceeds, output expands and with it efficiency increases and costs drop. The emergence of new technologies with scale economies can be thus rather useful in explaining new macroeconomic developments in the industrial economies.

2.4   Stability and large-scale production

Scale economies lead to increased vulnerability to shocks. An intuitive explanation is provided by contrasting the behavior of an industry with increasing returns with that of one with diminishing returns.

Consider an industry with diminishing returns to scale, the case typically discussed in textbooks. As output rises, efficiency falls and costs per unit rise. Consider now a drop in demand. Output decreases as well. At lower output levels productivity rises and this lowers costs and prices. The lower prices tend to restore the original level of demand, so that the initial drop in demand is offset.

A parallel argument shows that with decreasing returns an increase in demand is also self-correcting. As demand expands, output increases, and this raises costs and prices, thus checking further increases in demand.

A change in demand therefore sets in motion forces that tend to restore the original level. The system has built-in stability properties: Changes in demand, either upward or downward, tend to set in motion forces that restore the original level of demand and output. Changes from the original position are self-canceling.

With increasing returns, however, exactly the opposite is true. Increasing returns mean that efficiency rises as production expands, and thus costs fall. In this case a drop in demand, which lowers output, leads to a reduction rather than an increase in efficiency. This then leads to higher costs and higher prices. These higher prices naturally lead to a further reduction in demand. Thus a drop in demand sets in motion forces that lead to further decreases in demand and output. There is a self-reinforcing downward movement in economic activity.

With an expansion of demand, the opposite occurs: As output expands, productivity rises, lowering costs and prices and stimulating further demand increases. Again there is a tendency to reinforce a change, rather than to cancel it as in the case of diminishing returns. A drop in demand produces price changes that lead to further decreases, and an increase generates price changes conducive to further increases. The system is now unstable: It magnifies and amplifies changes, rather than canceling them.

The argument takes its simplest form in the case of an individual industry, but is easily generalized to the whole economy. It is therefore of interest that there is now substantial evidence that in many important sectors costs do indeed fall with scale.[4] The classical diminishing returns assumptions do not apply in these sectors.

In such a situation, consider an initial equilibrium, and suppose it to be disturbed by the loss of competitiveness on the part of one firm. Natural consequences are that this firm's market share falls and its output contracts. Now, as output contracts, costs will rise because the economies of large scale are reduced. The competitive position of this firm therefore worsens further, causing a further drop in output and a cycle of falling output and of rising costs. By this mechanism, then, a disturbance in an economy with falling costs is easily amplified. A decline in one firm's position sets in motion forces that worsen that decline and make it cumulative.

Note that, under the classical assumption of diminishing returns, just the opposite is true. Here a decline in a firm's competitive position, by cutting back its output and so reducing the incidence of diminishing returns, leads to a fall in costs and restores some of the lost competitiveness. With diminishing returns, there are therefore forces making for a return to the initial equilibrium, clearly the opposite of the increasing returns case.

The above arguments show that industrial structure is very sensitive to disturbance when there are economies of scale. A loss of competitiveness on the part of one firm sets in motion forces that reinforce that loss. In fact, the argument is quite symmetric: If one firm gains an advantage over its competitors, for example, through an innovation, then by expanding its market the firm reduces its costs further and reinforces the original gain, enabling it to move further ahead. There are thus tendencies that reinforce a lead, and increase a lag: If you get ahead of your competitors, you move further ahead, but if you get behind, then you trail more and more.

Similar arguments hold for the economy as a whole. Of course, the analysis is more complex in this case, as the economy will typically consist of a number of sectors, only some of which have economies of large-scale

---

[4] See the earlier footnote 1 and section 2.6.

production. However, it is generally the case that goods produced with economies of scale – consumer electronics and consumer durables for example – are leading sectors and constitute an important part of the market. They face demands that are highly income-elastic, whereas the diminishing-returns goods typically face demands with lower income elasticities. This has the important implication that an economic expansion will shift the pattern of demand toward the increasing-returns industries. Their costs and prices would then fall, leading to a further expansion of their demands, and so to a pattern of self-reinforcing growth for the economy as a whole.

Equally, a self-reinforcing contraction of the whole economy may occur in response to a drop in the demand faced by the increasing returns to scale sector. So at the aggregate macroeconomic level, expansion, whether due to domestic policies, to gains in overseas markets, or other factors, becomes self-reinforcing. Equally, contraction, due either to restrictive domestic policies or to loss of markets to foreign competitors, can become cumulative. The economy lacks the main self-correcting responses of markets with diminishing returns. This has substantial macroeconomic consequences, which are discussed in sections 2.5 and 2.6.[5]

2.5   Economic policies and large-scale technologies

Traditional macroeconomic policies can have unexpected effects with economies of scale. This is mainly because there is a different relationship between output levels and costs in the cases of increasing and of decreasing returns.

The level of output affects costs in two different ways: Through productivity, which changes with the scale of production, and through demand for factors, which also varies with output. Demand for factors influences factor prices and hence costs. In the case of increasing returns, these two effects act in opposite directions and tend to offset one another; in the case of diminishing returns, they act in unison and reinforce one another. Consequently, the economy's response to policies can be very different in the two cases.

Increasing returns reduce the effectiveness of traditional antiinflationary policies. The point here is that if the economy is in a period of contraction, then average productivity falls in the increasing returns sectors, raising their costs. On the other hand, recession reduces demand for factors and so will lower factor prices, which tends to lower costs. The net

---

[5] A detailed analysis of this issue, using more formal economic analysis, can be found in Chapter 9 and in G. M. Heal, "Macrodynamics and Returns to Scale," *Economic Journal* (in press).

impact of contraction on the price level will depend on the balance between these two effects: the drop in costs due to the reduction in demand for factors and in factor prices, and the rise in costs due to the loss of efficiency as output falls. If the latter predominates, then deflationary policies could actually lead to a combination of recession and inflation, the opposite of what is intended. If deflationary policies do succeed in stabilizing the price level, they will do so to a smaller degree than would be expected in a regime of diminishing returns. Severe deflation may be necessary to achieve price stability. In the diminishing returns case, of course, the effects of output on factor prices and on efficiency act in the same direction. A contraction of output raises efficiency, so that cost pressures are reduced both by efficiency gains and by reduced demand in factor markets.

A similar point can be made about an expansion: With increasing returns, if the economy is expanding, efficiency rises and reduces costs and prices. There will be an offsetting upward pressure on factor prices due to higher levels of demand. If the efficiency gains predominate, the outcome will be growth with price stability.

The crucial point here is that with economies of scale a contraction, by making production less efficient, can generate an upward pressure on costs and so begin an inflationary process. Expansion, however, tends naturally to reduce costs.

These conclusions are reminiscent of earlier discussions about the development of "vicious" and "virtuous" circles in macroeconomic performance. A number of commentators have noted[6] that both successes and failures tend to be self-reinforcing at the macroeconomic level, and have speculated on the possible causes of this. One line of argument sees the explanation in the behavior of investment: High growth rates encourage high levels of investment, which lead to a high rate of introduction of newer and more productive techniques. This strengthens a country's competitive position in the world economy, so reinforcing the high initial growth rate. Such an argument in no way conflicts with the one that we are advancing: Both imply that expansion reduces inflationary pressures, and that contraction may worsen them. The mechanisms are different, however, as are the detailed microeconomic implications.

2.6   Macroeconomic policies

The policy implications of this analysis are quite immediate. Inflationary pressures cannot easily be cured by traditional deflationary policies if economies of scale are important. Such policies reduce output further and

[6] See, for example, W. Beckerman et al. (1965), *The British Economy in 1975*, Cambridge University Press.

so lower efficiency and raise costs in the increasing returns sectors; in fact, they defeat some of their original purpose. Traditional deflationary policies will therefore incur all of the usual social costs of unemployment and wasted resources, but may in addition be of limited value in reducing inflation.

The social costs of deflation may be particularly high in industries with economies of scale. Industries with increasing returns will not contract continuously as demand falls. They will contract to some extent and then shut down completely, throwing large numbers of workers onto the labor market. The reason is that their profitability and competitiveness fall as they contract, so that they will usually go out of business before their market share falls to zero.[7] The only way of preventing this is to subsidize their output to sustain a sufficiently high level of demand to achieve efficiency. Situations of this type have clearly arisen in many OECD countries in such industries as steel, automobiles, and coal.

Another conventional argument for deflation is also invalid in this context: the supposed efficiency gains from increasing the competitive pressures under which an economy operates. The theory is that the resulting shake-out eliminates inefficiency, so that in the long run the competitive position of the economy is strengthened.

Again, it is clear that while there may be some efficiency gains from such a process, there will also be efficiency *losses* from the smaller scale of operation, as economies of large scale are forgone. The rationale for restrictive policies as a response to stagflation is thus weak in modern economies with large-scale technologies. Not only are the social costs in terms of unemployment very high, but such policies are of little value in reducing prices or raising efficiency in important sectors of the economy. If deflation is pursued by restrictive monetary policies, then the resultant high interest rates may lead to bankruptcies among the capital-intensive sectors of the economy, unless these are subsidized.

There is a positive side to this analysis, which is just the converse of the above. Appropriate expansionary policies, focused on increasing returns to scale sectors, will not only raise output and employment, but may also reduce inflationary pressures. A possible example is the current expansionary phase in the U.S. economy, which has been led by high-technology sectors. Expansionary policies need, therefore, to be oriented toward increased output in industries where there are scale economies, that is, typically to high-technology and to mass-production industries. What is required is selective and balanced expansion of supply and demand – for

---

[7] This point is developed formally in G. M. Heal and G. Chichilnisky, "Monetary Policies and Increasing Returns," Cowles Foundation Discussion Paper, Yale University, New Haven, 1982.

example, tax incentives for expenditure directed toward particular industries that hold the promise of higher productivity gains.

Will an overall demand expansion, the traditional Keynesian medicine, do the job? A general expansion of demand would meet these criteria only if increasing-returns goods had higher income elasticities of demand than others. Usually one would need to steer the extra expenditures toward appropriate sectors, using, for example, differential rates of sales tax by sector, or choosing to expand by monetary rather than fiscal policies if the activities in increasing returns sectors were highly sensitive to interest rates. In practice, the sectors with most scope for cost reduction via output expansion appear to be manufacturers of electric and electronic equipment, manufacturers of chemicals and allied products, transportation, communication, and vehicle production.[8]

2.7   The antitrust dilemma

We have placed considerable emphasis on the growing importance of economies of scale and on the implications that this has for macroeconomic policy. It also has implications for other aspects of policy, and in particular for the complex of policy issues relating to antitrust and antimonopoly policy, regulation, and industrial policy.

The notion underlying traditional antitrust policy is simple. It is that competition is conducive to efficiency, that many small firms form a more competitive environment than a few large ones, and that in consequence it is appropriate to discourage industrial concentration and to prevent the emergence of large and dominant firms.

In an environment where large-scale production is a prerequisite of efficiency, such an approach has to be refined. The preservation of a fragmented and competitive industrial structure may be inconsistent with a technically efficient organization of production.

This poses a difficult conflict for the policy maker. The options appear to be to preserve competition, with its possible advantages of flexibility, responsiveness to consumers' needs, and innovative capacity, or to allow domination of the market by a large but technically efficient organization. This dilemma is being increasingly recognized and, indeed, over the past decade many industrial countries have pursued a very ambivalent line on antitrust policy. Under the Labour governments of the 1960s, the United

---

[8] See H. Houthakker, *Brookings Papers on Economic Activity* no. 1, 1979. Also, A. F. Friedlander, C. Winston, and K. Wang, "Costs, Technology and Productivity in the U.S. Automobile Industry," *Bell Journal of Economics,* 14(1) (Spring 1983), 1–20, study the incidence of scale economics of the U.S. automobile industry and find them to be an important determinant of productivity and competitiveness.

Kingdom possessed both the Monopolies Commission, intended to preserve the competitive structure of industries, and an Industrial Reorganization Commission, whose purpose was to encourage interfirm mergers so as to make British industry more competitive on international markets. One can find similar instances in French economic policy.[9]

Although this conflict between competition and efficiency emerges naturally, it is not inevitable. The size of the market is crucial: If this is large enough, it will allow the existence of enough firms to provide effective competition, each producing at a large and efficient scale. However, if the minimum efficient scale of operation grows because of technical change, this balance could be destroyed. A simultaneous expansion of the market may be needed to allow many firms to remain in production at this enlarged scale.

In sum: Increasing returns and competition can coexist if the market expands rapidly as large-scale technologies develop. Such outcomes are certainly not impossible. Enhanced opportunities for economies of scale can lead to lower costs and prices, and thus to an expansion of demand. So if demand is sufficiently elastic, one may find increased-scale economies leading to a simultaneous expansion of all firms and of demand. There is some evidence that this occurred with the automobile industry until the 1960s, although since then there has been a clear worldwide tendency to concentration of this industry.[10] To a certain extent such simultaneous expansion has also occurred in segments of the electronics industry, an industry that exhibits increasing returns. However, such outcomes are more likely in periods of rising income levels, also more characteristic of the era prior to the 1970s.

2.8   New technologies and employment

A market expansion generated by the exploitation of economies of scale is what Adam Smith had in mind when he saw the extent of the market and the division of labor interacting to raise the wealth of nations.

It is worth noting that under such circumstances new technologies may lead to more rather than to less employment of labor. The expansion resulting from the increasing-returns technologies may indeed be accom-

---

[9] Considerable debate accompanied recent legal attempts in the United States to break up large firms in communications and electronics. In addition, the Microelectronics and Computer Corporation, a joint venture among high-technology firms, has been granted antitrust exemption in order to improve the international competitive position of the U.S. industry (*Washington Post,* 11 May 1983, p. D7). More general changes are under consideration by the Justice Department (*Washington Post,* 30 March 1983, p. D8).

[10] See Harvard Business School, *Note on the International Automobile Industry,* 9-380-086, 1979.

panied by an increase in the level of employment, even though the new technologies are labor-saving. A necessary condition for this rise in employment as labor-saving technologies emerge is that demand and output expand sufficiently fast. This obviously happened as a result of the introduction of labor-saving technologies in the industrial revolution and in response to the introduction of mass production of vehicles in the 1920s and 1930s.

Whether or not a simultaneous expansion of employment and labor-saving technologies can occur under present circumstances is an empirical question, and one whose answer may be amenable to influence by appropriate policies. However, economic theory gives a clear answer on this point: In the standard models of market economies, employment can indeed rise after the introduction of labor-saving technologies, provided the appropriate conditions are met.

In cases where it is not possible to reconcile scale economies and competition through expansion of the market, several policy options are available. One is to encourage domestic concentration to the levels required for production efficiency and then to remove all import restrictions, relying on international competition to prevent the large domestic producer from exploiting its dominant position in the home market. Of course, this option is not available for goods or services that cannot readily be traded internationally, such as telecommunications, transportation, gas, or electricity. There are also certain sectors for which it might be held to be unsuitable on security grounds, if the preservation of a domestic industrial capacity is believed to be of strategic importance. In such cases, a traditional approach is to regulate the industry concerned.

2.9   Regulation and increasing returns

The precise institutional structure under which regulation occurs varies from country to country. Its essence, however, is always the same: control over price, output, and investment decisions to prevent the exploitation of monopoly power and to ensure an efficient allocation of resources. There are a number of alternative approaches to this, which differ largely in the extent to which the regulated enterprise is assumed to be self-financing or to be able to draw on subsidies out of general tax revenues.

On grounds of economic efficiency, the preferred regulatory policy has traditionally been marginal-cost pricing: Having prices at or near marginal costs is a prerequisite for efficient resource allocation. However, with economies of scale, marginal cost is less than average cost, so that such a policy leads to revenues that do not cover average costs, and so to losses. If subsidies are not available, such an approach is ruled out.

An alternative approach, often referred to as "Ramsey pricing,"[11] seeks a pricing policy that comes nearest to marginal-cost pricing and to efficiency, subject to a constraint that no subsidy is required in this case.

In recent years there has been considerable dissatisfaction with both of these approaches. There has in fact been a remarkable coincidence of theoretical and of institutional and policy-oriented viewpoints here. Recent theoretical advances in our understanding of markets with increasing returns have made it clear that marginal-cost pricing is a less attractive policy than was previously believed, and that the attainment of efficiency with increasing returns is a particularly challenging task. An interesting point to have emerged is that, with increasing returns, the possibility of achieving economic efficiency is sensitive to the distribution of income: Not all income distributions are compatible with efficiency.[12] This contrasts with the standard results of welfare economies with decreasing returns, where considerations of equity and efficiency are completely independent.

Simultaneous with these theoretical advances, there has also been widespread dissatisfaction with existing modes of regulation at the political level, and a feeling that these have produced organizations that are neither efficient nor innovative and responsive. This has led in the United States to deregulation in such fields as air transport and telecommunications; in the United Kingdom it has led to the privatization of industries that were previously state-owned, such as British Telecom. All of this has led to a critical reevaluation of policies for the management of increasing-returns sectors and to attempts to devise policies and institutions that combine the safeguards of regulation with the advantages of a competitive environment.

One possibility is to have a market served primarily by a large regulated enterprise and then, in addition, to allow private firms to compete with this. This was in fact, the position of the U.S. telecommunications industry for the few years prior to the divestiture of AT&T. Unfortunately there is one major drawback to such a system: It can lead to what is known as "creamskimming," which arises as follows. If there is a dominant regulated enterprise serving a market, then the regulators will set prices for this that they believe to be conducive to an efficient use of resources – prices typically related to the "Ramsey prices" referred to above. If, as is likely, the enterprise produces several different products, then such pric-

---

[11] See, for example, M. Boiteux, "On the Management of Public Monopolies Subject to Budget Constraints," *Journal of Economic Theory* 3 (September 1971), 219–40 and W. Baumol and D. Bradford, "Optimal Departures from Marginal Cost Pricing," *American Economic Review* 60(3) (1970), 265–83.

[12] For details of this case, see Donald J. Brown and Geoffrey Heal, "Equity, Efficiency and Increasing Returns," *Review of Economic Studies* 46 (1979), 1571–85.

ing rules will generally involve losses on some products and profits on others, with the mix as a whole breaking even. Under such circumstances, it is clear what will be the policies of private competitors: They will compete on the profitable product lines, but not on the others, and will be able to undercut the regulated firm, not having to earn enough profit to cover losses on other lines. Such creamskimming is, of course, exactly what happened in the U.S. telecommunication industry in the early 1980s, when new long-distance carriers entered the market for long-distance telephone services in competition with AT&T. They were able to undercut AT&T in this market because they were not regulated in the same way and so had no obligation to cross-subsidize short-distance services.

The disadvantage of such creamskimming is that it eventually leads to goods being traded for prices quite different from those set by the regulators, and so undermines their attempt to set prices conducive to efficient patterns of consumption and production. Prices fall for the goods on which the regulated firm makes a profit, because of competition from the private entrants, and then rise on the others, because the regulated firm is left selling only these and so cannot sustain loss-making prices for them.

An ideal system would face consumers with prices that lead to efficient patterns of resource use when there are increasing returns, while also allowing enough competition to ensure an incentive to innovate and to remain responsive to consumers' interests. Such a system can, in fact, be devised. It involves the use of excise taxes on the regulated goods and services. The effect of such a tax is that the amount that a consumer pays for the good or service differs from that which the producer receives, so that one can think of consumers and producers as facing different prices. Within this approach, it is possible to choose the prices received by producers so that they avoid creamskimming and so can be sustained[13] even in the face of competition and entry. At the same time, the prices faced by consumers can be chosen so as to encourage efficient patterns of consumption and production. Furthermore, it can be shown that these two price systems can always be chosen so that the total payments made by consumers just equal the totals received by producers; thus, in aggregate, there would be no net taxation or subsidization, and the system would be self-supporting.[14]

In an environment where increasing returns are becoming increasingly

[13] The concept of *sustainable* prices is discussed for example, in, G. Faulhaber, "Cross-Subsidization: Pricing in Public Enterprises,"*American Economic Review* 65 (1975), 966–77.
[14] For details, see Donald J. Brown and Geoffrey Heal, "The Optimality of Regulated Pricing: A General Equilibrium Analysis," Cowles Foundation Discussion Paper no. 684, December, 1983, Yale University, New Haven.

important, there are clearly great attractions in an institutional framework that makes as much use as possible of competition while recognizing that perfectly competitive markets are unattainable and that competition alone will not ensure an efficient pattern of consumption and production. The scheme just outlined is a regulated environment that allows competition: Regulation takes care of overall economic efficiency, and competition encourages innovation, cost consciousness, and attention to consumers.

CHAPTER 3

Protectionism and the management of trade

3.1   Protectionism in industrial countries

The recent recession in the industrial countries has been the worst since the Great Depression of the 1930s. Unemployment and the decline in competitiveness of traditional sectors led industrial countries to protect their industries from international competition. In the United States the high value of the dollar added fuel to the protectionist mood. As foreign goods became less expensive in dollar terms they displaced domestic goods, leading to a large balance-of-payments deficit and to further pressures for protection.

Only in a few cases has this recent wave of protectionism taken the form of explicit tariffs or quotas. More often, there have been informal agreements to restrict competition – for example, voluntary restrictions on the number of Japanese cars imported into the United States and the United Kingdom, and the suggested harmonization of the prices of food exports from Europe and the United States.[1]

A consequence of protection has been increased emphasis on the establishment of foreign manufacturing facilities in countries that were previously only export markets. For example, Japanese corporations have recently established numerous plants in Europe and the United States. The output of these plants then avoids the protective barriers erected around the local market.

The development of foreign manufacturing facilities in industrial countries has in turn led to the discussion and promotion of "local content" laws. These laws, if approved, would imply that to avoid the measures introduced to protect the local market, it is not sufficient for a foreign firm to manufacture a good locally: It must in addition *purchase* locally a certain fraction of the inputs for this good. The aim is, of course, to prevent the plant from simply importing components from its parent factory abroad and assembling them locally. This practice is not new; it

---

[1] This has been documented for example, by UNCTAD. A 1981 UNCTAD report comments that "there has been a decline in the importance of fixed measures of protection, especially custom duties. . . . There is now greater reliance upon mechanisms of flexible protection, under which restrictions or other measures can be applied when specific conditions exist" [UNCTAD, Doc. To/B (XXIII) Sc. I/Mics, para. 4].

has been used in developing countries for many years, and has been criticized as decreasing the competitive environment of their economies. Complex protective measures that are neither taxes nor quotas are sometimes referred to as "orderly marketing arrangements." They are often justified as ways of ensuring "fair trade." Indeed, a recent, widely quoted statement, made in the context of U.S. – European negotiations on European steel exports to the United States, was that "there is no such thing as free trade in steel: what we're trying to obtain is fair trade."[2]

The words "fair trade" appear often in this context. However often they are used, we have so far no definition for them. There is only an intuitive feeling that the market needs to be protected against manipulation or "unfair practices." Expressions of concern for "fair trade" are often little more than attempts to give a veneer of respectability to a protectionist lobby. However, underlying the rhetoric, there are substantive issues that deserve our attention.

The range of policy interventions in markets utilized by governments has increased greatly, often undermining competitive practices. In addition to tariffs and quotas, which are in principle controlled by agreements such as GATT, we find export subsidies, regulatory practices that give an advantage to domestic firms, and indirect subsidies via government involvement in research and development, to mention only a few. Calls for fair trade often emerge in response to the proliferation of such practices, which are viewed as subjecting other producers to unfair competition.[3]

In view of current policies toward the export sector, the traditional economic dichotomy between open and closed economies has lost much of its meaning. We are used to measuring a country's position with respect to the international market by reference to two polar cases: (1) the open or liberal economy with no trade restrictions and with an extensive participation in international markets, and (2) the closed economy with trade restrictions and minimal involvement in trade. This classification seems inadequate in the present economic environment. A country with a small number of substantive but carefully selected trade restrictions may participate more actively in the international economy than one with a uniformly low level of restrictions or with none at all. Indeed, Japan is an example of a country that is a major participant in the international market and that has had stringent restrictions in certain sectors. Korea and Taiwan are also export-oriented and active participants in the inter-

---

[2] The quote is from Harry Holiday, chairperson of Armco Inc., as reported in the New York Times, 23 April, 1984. A related theme can be found in William Safire's article entitled, "Free Trade Is Dandy, but the U.S. Should Also Demand Fair Trade," in the New York Times, 8 May, 1984.

[3] There is a review of such measures, and of their legal status, in G. C. Hufbauer and J. S. Erb, Subsidiaries in International Trade, Institute for International Economics, Washington, D.C., 1984

national economy that have carefully controlled export sectors. Amartya Sen notes[4] that no states outside of the socialist block have ever exercised the same degree of control over their economic resources as have Korea and Taiwan. On the other side, Chile adopted a traditional open trading policy in the 1970s and early 1980s, but has not increased its participation in international markets. More liberal policies do not necessarily mean more trade.

There is another reason why the distinction between liberal and protected economies is no longer particularly informative. A fully liberal trading regime used to be associated with balanced and efficient trade patterns. However, with the emergence of new technologies, this association has been weakened. Protectionism does not provide efficient outcomes either. There is an obvious need for new concepts, and the interest in fair and orderly trade reflects this need.

In this context, the merits and limitations of liberal trading regimes need to be reexamined. The most persuasive case in favor of a liberal trading regime is that which was provided by classical theories of international trade, and we shall use it as a point of departure.

3.2   Economic background: the classical theory

Classical theories explain that trade arises from comparative advantages and leads to efficient outcomes. Different regions have different endowments of factors – capital, labor, and other productive inputs – and thus can produce goods at different costs. If trade stems from such differences, then all countries are better off with free trade than with no trade.

The traditional picture of comparative advantages gives a good explanation, for example, of why the United States exports food, whereas the United Kingdom imports it: The United States has relatively more land and can therefore produce at lower costs. It is generally recognized, however, that comparative advantages cannot explain as well why Europe imports, and the United States exports, computers and aircraft, or why Japan exports automobiles and electronics to other industrial countries. Such trade has little to do with comparative advantages in the traditional sense, and much more to do with who entered the field first, whose research and development programs have been most successful, and who has managed to get costs further down by mass production and the successful exploitation of economies of scale.[5]

In any case, under certain conditions one can show that all countries

---

[4] "Level of Poverty: Policy and Change," World Bank Staff Working Paper no. 401, July 1980.
[5] This point is made in William R. Cline, *"Reciprocity," A New Approach to World Trade Policy,* Institute for International Economics, Washington, D.C., 1982.

gain, or at least do not lose, from trade. More can be said yet about competitive international markets. The "invisible hand," an informal term for the market adjustment process, leads under appropriate conditions to prices at which markets clear and to efficiency in the distribution of economic resources. This is a classical result that summarizes the optimality property of competitive markets; however, it is not always properly understood.

Efficiency, also known as Pareto efficiency, means that no redistribution of resources can make some individual better off without someone else being worse off. Under certain conditions on the technologies, efficiency is also associated with the maximization of profits. It is worth noting that under the appropriate conditions no intervention is needed to achieve such market clearing and efficiency: These are the natural outcomes of the free working of market forces.[6]

With this background, we can now state that "fair trade" usually alludes to trading practices that are consistent with competitive markets and thus could lead to optimal outcomes. Unfair competition typically refers to practices that are inconsistent with competitive markets and thus may hinder the achievement of optimal market outcomes. For example, low import prices achieved by foreign governments' intervention are deemed to be artificial and to hinder the competitive behavior of markets.

A confusion arises because, for certain imports such as extractive resources, the problem is seen to be the opposite: The typical complaint is that import prices are too high, not too low. It is not a priori clear why in the case of some imports high prices constitute a problem, whereas in the case of others it is low prices that are the problem. Certainly it is not that Japanese cars compete with domestic production whereas OPEC oil does not. In both the United Kingdom and the United States oil imports compete with domestic production: In all industrial countries they com-

---

[6] Great caution is required when interpreting the statement that the free working of the market forces leads to equilibrium and to efficiency. This statement might be interpreted as saying that when prices adjust freely to supply and demand (decreasing with increases in the former and increasing with increases in the latter), then an equilibrium will be established in which Pareto efficiency prevails. This latter statement is in fact false in most competitive market economies, simply because many such economies are not stable, so that typical price adjustments to supply and demand of the type mentioned above do *not* lead to market clearing. The correct interpretation is that, with an appropriate formalization of a competitive market economy (see K. J. Arrow and F. H. Hahn, *General Competitive Analysis,* North-Holland, Amsterdam/NY, 1971) and with appropriate conditions (which exclude increasing returns), there exist prices that clear markets and lead to Pareto-efficient allocations. *How* the economy gets there is a completely different matter, about which not much is known.

pete with coal, as well as with other substitutes that are inputs to production, such as labor and capital. We shall return to this point later, but it seems clear that fair competition cannot be characterized only by the level of import prices. The level of prices is but a "proxy" for the main economic concern: the appropriate functioning of markets. Fair and orderly trade must therefore be related to the *optimality* properties of markets. The issue is whether trade and pricing policies are in some sense conducive to market clearing and macroeconomic efficiency, as well as to an efficient distribution of resources.

3.3 Efficient trade and economies of scale

We noted in section 3.2 that under certain conditions the invisible hand leads to trade balance and to an efficient allocation of resources. We also noted that classical theories of international trade seem to give a good explanation of certain types of trade (for example, in food), but not of others (trade in certain industrial products).[7] These two observations are related. The conditions under which the invisible hand can be shown to work satisfactorily are extremely strong. In technical terms, they involve a convexity requirement on production possibilities: This rules out any degree of increasing returns to scale or to proportions, and also any economies of scope, that is, of the joint production of several products. One can gain a feeling for the stringency of this condition by remarking that any fixed costs of production, however small, are incompatible with the conditions assumed in establishing that the invisible hand works satisfactorily.

Economies of scale are clearly significant in many fields that are important in international trade; indeed, this is typically the case in precisely those areas where traditional trade theory seems most lacking in explanatory power. Examples have already been mentioned in Chapter 2 – computers, aircraft, automobiles, and electronics. In all of these cases, there are reasons why large-scale production leads to lower costs. The reasons may be purely technological, or may derive from the high fixed costs of research and development, as in the case of computers, or may be partly managerial and organizational, as with automobiles and with the information industries.[8] In any event, classical trade theory assumes away all such effects, and this is a crucial step in its ability to derive the well-

---

[7] For a review of alternatives to the classical theories, see Paul Krugman, "New Theories of Trade Amongst Industrial Countries," *American Economic Association Papers and Proceedings,* 1983; published in American Economic Review 73(2) (1983), 343–7.
[8] See footnotes 1 and 2 of Chapter 2 for a more detailed discussion.

known propositions about market clearing, Pareto efficiency, and gains from trade. The distortionary effects and welfare losses associated with market interventions such as tariffs and quotas are also demonstrated under the assumption of decreasing returns to scale.

When scale economies in production are taken into account, the applicability of the classical theory is greatly limited. If one admits increasing returns to scale, the usual conclusions about the gains from unrestricted trade and the working of the invisible hand must be heavily qualified. In particular, a concept of "orderly trade" emerges naturally. This is because there are conditions under which active management of trade flows is needed to ensure that markets clear and that all countries gain[9]: The invisible hand no longer suffices.

In an international economy with increasing returns, all of the gains from free trade may accrue to just one trading partner, with the others possibly even being net losers. Active management of trade flows may be required to ensure market clearing and Pareto efficiency. This typically involves carefully coordinated limits on imports or on exports, or some mutually agreed -upon and compensating transfers from the gainer to the loser.

A framework thus emerges within which one can evaluate alternative trade policies and find some analytical equivalents to such phrases as "undue market penetration" or "unfair competition."[10] Both of these phrases will still refer to deviations from market clearing and efficient allocations, but these will now be compared to the efficient or market-clearing outcomes arising from managed trade, rather than from free competition.

It is important to differentiate between *managed trade* and *protectionism*. These two terms are very different indeed, the former being a far more constructive approach to international economic relations. In sections 3.5 and 3.6 we analyze the implications of managed trade for economies with increasing returns and show that, although protectionism prevents specialization and limits trade, managed trade may in some cases encourage specialization and allow trade to expand. In order to do this, we now look in more detail at the working of the invisible hand in markets with economies of scale.

---

[9] For a discussion of such conditions, see Chapter 10, which presents a more formal theoretical background to this chapter.

[10] Interestingly, this point is suggested in UNCTAD document TD/B (XXIII) Sc. I/Misc. 1 GE. 81-55447. Paragraph 14 refers to the idea that countries have a right to maintain "minimum viable production" as a justification for managing trade; but the concept of a minimum viable scale of production presupposes economies of scale in production. In this case it refers to a level of production large enough to make costs competitive.

3.4   The invisible hand with large-scale technologies

It is often overlooked that, with scale economies in production, there may be no prices at which it is possible for all partners to gain from trade and also for trade to balance. This may hold even when prices are fully flexible and markets perfectly competitive. With scale economies in production, price adjustments in response to market forces may not be able to balance supply and demand, even when markets are stable.[11]

The conclusion is then that to achieve both gains from trade and the balance between supply and demand we may need a "visible hand": The "invisible hand" or price adjustments that follow supply and demand are unable to do this work adequately. The management of prices, of trade flows, or of a combination of both may be needed to achieve efficiency and to clear markets at the same time.

The argument bears a little elaboration. Consider two countries and two produced goods, each of which is manufactured under conditions of economies of scale. Each country produces most efficiently by specializing in one good and meeting its needs for the other by trade: If each country were to produce all of its requirements of both products, this would lead to smaller scale and thus to less efficient production. Productive efficiency thus requires specialization in trade, with each country exporting the good in which it specializes, and importing the other. This is a familiar argument, and one that certainly applies to economies of scale. However, this argument neglects an important point.

The point is that we have looked so far only at the supply side of the problem rather than at overall feasibility. From the point of view of supply or productive efficiency, it would be desirable to specialize and trade. But is this feasible? Will there be a market for the goods thus produced? This is, of course, a crucial question. Without such a market, producers would not be able to sell their products, and the output levels that are a priori productively efficient would not be produced.

Specialization is thus only feasible if the international market can clear: that is, if at the market prices the amount that each country wishes to export of the good in which it has specialized just equals what the other one wishes to import. This sounds like a remarkable coincidence, and indeed it is. It can be shown rigorously that this coincidence does occur in markets with constant or decreasing returns: This is one of the striking

---

[11] See, for example, the discussion of economies of scale in K. J. Arrow and F. H. Hahn, *General Competitive Analysis,* North-Holland, Amsterdam. The issue is also studied in G. M. Heal, "Stable Disequilibrium Prices," Cowles Foundation Discussion Paper no. 650, Yale University, New Haven, November 1982, and G. M. Heal, "Rational Rationing and Increasing Returns," *Economic Letters,* 8(1) (1981), 19–27. See also Chapter 10.

roles of the invisible hand. However, in markets with increasing returns to scale this is not a typical outcome. With scale economies in production, price adjustments may not equate demands and supplies and ensure that markets clear. No matter how flexible prices are, a free market equilibrium may therefore fail to exist, and the potential gains from specialization may never be realized.

Intuitively, the reason for this failure is that the level of production of an industry with economies of scale does not adjust continuously in response to price movements or to shifts in demand. It typically changes in quantum jumps, and thus may persistently fail to match demand. For a given set of prices, there is a level of production below which it is not efficient or profitable for such industries to operate. At such prices demand may be smaller than this minimum level of output and, if production were to take place at this minimum level, there would be excess supply, which is obviously not a sustainable outcome. With scale economies it may not be profitable for producers to meet low levels of demand, a problem that does not emerge with decreasing returns to scale. The alternative is for producers not to produce at all: Intermediate outcomes lead to losses. If producers do not produce, however, we have excess demand: Markets do not clear either.

In the case of production with diminishing returns, as prices change, demand shifts up and down in small increments. By contrast, the increasing-returns firm can only produce either above a minimum efficient level of output, or at zero. The market thus jumps from excess supply to excess demand as prices change and the producer switches between somewhere above the minimum feasible output and zero output. The market may thus remain persistently in a disequilibrium position. This cannot happen in decreasing-returns economies, because there supply adjusts continuously to changes in demand and prices: The requirement of positive profits places no minimum constraint on output.

Consider as an example the trading relationship between the United States and Japan. It is characterized by a persistent U.S. need to face the Japanese with quantitative constraints on their exports if trade between the two countries is to be held in balance, or even in an acceptable degree of imbalance. The constraints are "voluntary quotas" typically imposed on goods whose production is characterized by increasing returns, namely automobiles and consumer electronics. The position is made more complicated by Japan's unwillingness to accompany a trade surplus by encouraging a capital outflow.

Another example may be the excess demand for industrial goods that are exported from industrial to developing countries and produced under increasing returns. A measure of this excess demand is given by the persistent balance-of-payments deficits of the importers.

3.5   Management and protectionism

Trade management as defined here may be quite different from other forms of market intervention such as protectionism. Protectionism is designed specifically to prevent specialization that would naturally occur as a result of market forces. An example is the Multifiber Agreement, which seeks to delay the trend toward the specialization of the textile industry in developing countries, which presumably offer better prices and products. This agreement attempts to prevent or reduce specialization. Less explicit policies of this sort exist in other industries such as steel and various light manufactures. The point of protectionism is frequently to protect inefficient industries from competition, and it generally does this by reducing trade.

In contrast to protectionism, our vision of managed trade would aid market clearing and promote overall efficiency, thus leading to optimal outcomes in markets where the invisible hand cannot ensure such outcomes. In certain cases this procedure may lead to more rather than less specialization, and to more trade rather than to less.

Efficiency may require appropriate policies to phase out rather than to protect obsolete parts of an industry. An example is the European policy toward steel, where incentives are offered to ease the phasing out of plants in sectors of the industry that have a large minimum efficient scale of operation and cannot compete with Taiwan or Korea, while encouraging the production of more specialist products. This case shows clearly the difference between managed trade and protectionism, and illustrates the fact that managed trade policies cannot be formulated in isolation from other domestic policies. Indeed, the management of trade should be seen as a natural extension of existing sector-specific policies[12] to the international arena.

In general, as our examples suggest, a coherent managed trade policy would not involve techniques or institutions that on their own are fundamentally novel; rather, it would involve the coordinated application of existing domestic policies to those sectors of the economy that are involved in international trade – of course, on the understanding that such

---

[12] Such policies are often referred to as "industrial targeting." For a more detailed discussion, see P. Krugman, "The U.S. Response to Foreign Industrial Targeting," *Brookings Papers on Economic Activity*, 1 (1984), 77 – 121 and G. C. Hufbauer and J. S. Erb, *Subsidies in International Trade*, Institute for International Economics, Washington, D.C., 1984, pp. 107 – 9.

policies are well designed and efficiently implemented, which has certainly not always been the case in the past.

Regulatory techniques of the type described in Chapter 2, involving competition as well as regulation, could be applied to the international sector as well as to purely domestic sectors. Of course, this would require overall consistency of policies as well as an internationally agreeable set of rules and practices, which would be a modification and extension of the existing framework, the General Agreement on Trade and Tariffs (GATT). Indeed, with increasing government involvement in and encouragement of high-technology and export-oriented industries,[13] there is clearly a need for a revision of the institutional framework governing international trade to define acceptable goals and limits for this involvement. Such a revision will automatically constitute a definition of trade policy: It will be crucial to ensure that it is developed with reference to the issues discussed above.

3.6   Trade policy in a North–South context

The statements made so far about the desirability of specialization with increasing returns may not be applicable to North–South trade due to fundamental asymmetry between the traders. North–South Trade consists typically of increasing-returns products being exported in exchange for decreasing-returns products. An example is the trade of industrial goods, which are often produced under increasing returns, for labor-intensive manufactures or primary products, which are produced with decreasing returns. This fundamental asymmetry has several economic consequences, and management of North–South trade may thus have to take quite a different form. Indeed, one may have to recommend against many forms of specialization that were suggested for the industrial countries trading among themselves.

Consider the problem of an exporter of a decreasing-returns product trading with an exporter of an increasing-returns product. A higher volume of trade increases the efficiency of the exporter with increasing returns and the productivity of its labor, thus leading to domestic gains for the exporting country. At the international level, the increasing-returns exporter will also gain provided the higher volume of trade brings it higher revenues. The relative prices of the two goods traded, that is, the "terms of trade" of the traders, are the determining factor.

It may seem a priori that as trade expands the price of the increasing-returns product exported by the North will fall, and that the price of the decreasing-returns product will rise. This would be true if prices followed

---

[13] For documentation, see Hufbauer and Erb, op. cit.

costs (and input prices were constant): An expansion of output would lead to lower costs in the North, which has increasing returns, and to higher costs in the South, which has decreasing returns to scale. In such cases the expansion of trade would always lead to an improvement in terms of trade of the South vis-à-vis the North. However, quite the opposite may happen: An expansion of trade may worsen the terms of trade of the South under these circumstances. How could this come about?

An answer can be provided by following the rationale of W. Arthur Lewis's model of development. This would predict that trade expansion will cause a drop in the South's terms of trade if the North trades an increasing-returns good for a decreasing-returns product from the South. The reason is that in Lewis's model the relative prices of the traded products are determined by the *factoral terms of trade,* namely, the ratio of labor productivities in the two regions. Increased trade in these circumstances always improves the North's factoral terms of trade because it raises the productivity of labor in the North and lowers this in the South.

Such a drop in the South's terms of trade following an export expansion is also predicted within a general equilibrium model of North–South trade with competitive markets, a model discussed in detail in Chapters 4 and 11. The point is that if the South has abundant labor and dual technologies (two characteristics discussed in those chapters), then the expansion of exports can only occur with a contraction of domestic consumption. Such a contraction makes more products available to the international market, and this occurs at lower domestic wages, lower employment, and lower domestic production.

Under these circumstances, nothing could be more inefficient for the South than an expansion of labor-intensive exports. Any form of managed trade that seeks overall efficiency will advise against specialization in such cases.

It should be noted, however, that when a trade expansion is accompanied by increases in labor productivity in the South, and labor is more skilled and less "abundant," specialization need no longer have the negative impacts described above. This is discussed in Chapter 4. These points illustrate once again the importance of coordinating domestic and international policies, and exhibit rather clearly how an optimal management of trade will depend on the characteristics of the trading regions.

3.7 Structural change and new technologies in a changing economic environment

In an evolving economic environment, the ability of an economy to adjust to change is crucial to its success. Yet the very reasons that ensure the supremacy of industrial nations in the international order, their productivity and technological innovation, lead to inflexibilities and strains in their economies. The less productive and less innovative developing countries have a compensating virtue: They can adapt faster to a changing environment. The argument hinges on the importance of increasing returns in the capital-rich industrial countries. Both trade imbalances and inadequate structural flexibility are associated with their economies of scale.

With scale economies, it is only when operating at high output levels that a firm is efficient and productive. In this case, it becomes impossible to ensure the gradual contraction of declining industries and the gradual expansion of their successors. The difficulty arises because productivity increases with the scale of operation, and conversely decreases when this scale is reduced. This means that, once an industry is uncompetitive and unprofitable, any contraction will reduce its productivity and make its position deteriorate further. Since contraction is a natural consequence of an uncompetitive position, there is a vicious circle of decline here. Loss of competitive position leads to contraction, which leads to further loss of competitive position, and so on. Only through expansion could the firm with scale economies break out of this cycle, but expansion is emphatically *not* a natural consequence of loss of competitiveness. Such expansion would therefore require some "visible hand" to overcome the natural outcome of market forces. Because of the risks involved, and the public good aspects of the problem, policy intervention may be optimal.[14]

This phenomenon should be contrasted with the traditional case of diminishing returns and diseconomies of large-scale operations. In this case, productivity rises as output is cut back. Small-scale production avoids the diseconomies of large scales. Under these conditions, an uncompetitive industry will naturally reduce its scale. This will then raise its productivity, and help to restore its competitive position: The firm is "leaner but fitter." A loss of competitiveness therefore sets in motion forces that tend to compensate for this loss, and to restore the original position, rather than forces that lead to cumulative decline. In the case of diminishing returns, industrial structures have a degree of inherent stability and will change smoothly. In the case of increasing returns, they may be innately unstable and respond erratically to changes in the economic

---

[14] A firm whose costs fall with output, and that is faced with a loss of market share, has only one alternative to cutting back production and facing a further loss of market because of rises in costs: This is to expand output substantially, in the hope of reducing costs enough to reclaim a market share, enabling it to stay competitive. Such a policy clearly involves risks; it is typically costly, and its success depends upon the measures taken by competitors. However, the risk can be greatly reduced if there is a simultaneous expansion of total demand by, for example, fiscal or monetary measures, so that the probability of larger sales will be increased.

environment. As we saw in Chapter 2, they may also amplify the effects of external shocks and so make the transition to a new technology an economically costly and difficult operation. This tends to occur more often in older industrial countries with a large number of increasing-returns sectors, thus helping to explain why the newly industrializing countries can adapt faster and thrive in a changing world environment, as they have indeed done in the past decade.

3.8   Conclusions

We have shown that the technical improvements in industrial economies that led to greater efficiency and productivity also led to instability and increased costs of adjustment. Persistent trade imbalances and problems of structural adjustment both have roots in changes in technology that have led to the greater competitive efficiency of large-scale organization. This provides another approach to the issues of "fair competition" and "orderly trade." Both of these issues appear in the search for trade patterns that are conducive to trade balance and permit efficient production patterns, and that lead to industrial adjustments that minimize social costs. These patterns will typically not emerge from market forces, but will require conscious and selective intervention.

The ultimate conclusion from this analysis is that, short of abandoning the great benefits of new technologies, one cannot recommend, as an objective of international policy, a return to the pursuit of a trade regime as uniformly liberal as possible. With increasing returns, the invisible hand cannot ensure harmonious and efficient outcomes. Newer technologies have great potential payoffs, but require more sophisticated forms of social organization. There is a need for institutions that facilitate patterns of trade consistent with balanced markets and with the smooth occurrence of any necessary structural changes.

International economic policies must be coherent with domestic economic structures, especially when the trading economies exhibit increasing returns to scale. For developing countries this means a realistic appraisal of the limits on export prospects for many of their labor-intensive products or raw materials. This is elaborated further in Chapters 4 and 7.

For industrial countries, more sophisticated and realistic policies toward the new large-scale technologies are needed. The major technological innovations of our times require increased sophistication of our economic institutions. With increasing returns, unaided markets cannot be expected to perform perfectly.

Our institutions, including international markets, must evolve and adapt to the changing economic environment.

PART II

The role of developing countries

CHAPTER 4

Export strategies

4.1   The promotion of traditional exports

The past fifteen years have seen an increasing emphasis on development strategies based on the promotion of traditional exports. Such strategies have become an automatic policy recommendation by international organizations. The expansion of exports is one of the conditions that international agencies such as the IMF require for extending or refinancing loans to developing countries, accompanied by austerity measures and wage controls.[1]

Expanding the country's earnings by selling more to the international market is indeed an appealing prospect for countries with balance-of-payments deficits, foreign exchange constraints, or debt problems. However, there is widespread concern that the current economic climate in the industrial countries, which are the principal importers, is not propitious for a substantial expansion of exports of traditional commodities from developing countries.[2] It is also argued that even if such an export expan-

---

[1] The promotion of exports has been widely recommended, for example, by the World Bank and the IMF in recent years. See, for instance, World Development Reports 1980–3. The World Bank Vice-President for Research, Ann Krueger, has often presented export promotion as the most important element in a successful development strategy. This recommendation is based on empirical research performed for the National Bureau of Economic Research in which she strongly endorses export promotion for developing countries. A recent IMF publication by Managing Director, J. de Larosière states: "The objective of the Fund programs in these countries is to achieve a better balance of payments equilibrium in the medium term and a more efficient use of scarce resources by introducing a number of incentives and measures to generate more domestic savings, more investment, and more exports. . . . The Fund's role is to say: in view of the external financial resources available to you, the objective of restoring a viable balance of payments position within a reasonable period implies that you must limit your domestic consumption, increase your domestic savings, and expand your exports." See J. de Larosière, "Does the Fund Impose Austerity?" IMF, Washington, D.C., June 1984.

[2] The same point is made in "Trade and Development Report 1981: Report by the UNCTAD Secretariat," UNCTAD/TDR/2, United Nations Publication, Sales no. E.82.II.D.12. See in particular vol. I, p. 1, para. 1: "This year's *Trade and Development Report*. . . . reports on the serious deepening of the crisis in development. . . . and on the further deterioration of the international economic environment." See also p. 7: "Slower growth in the developed market-economy countries is curtailing directly their import demand and is also associated with structural changes in those countries which have a further negative impact on demand." There is also a reference there to "the progressive alteration of the international environment in ways that narrow the range of feasible policies open to developing countries to promote their own development, and that reduce the effectiveness of those that are available." Volume II, para. 3, also refers to

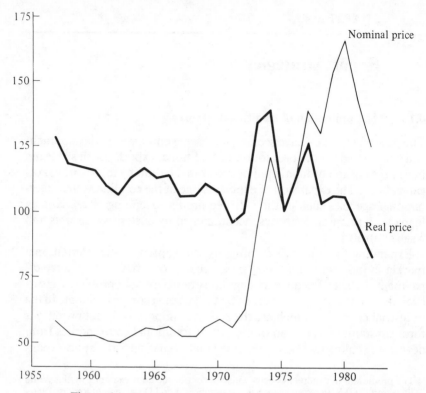

Figure 4.1. Nonoil commodity prices in nominal terms and in real terms. *Source*: data from World Bank, *World Development Report, 1984*.

sion were possible, it would require a sizable drop in real export prices. This would mean a drop in the South's terms of trade, which could lead to lower real wages, lower domestic consumption, and perhaps even lower export revenues. Export-led policies thus appear to be unrealistic, or even counterproductive. Are such concerns justified?

If we look at the goods exported by developing to industrial countries, the large majority still fall into two categories: primary commodities, such as copper, jute, or sugar, and labor-intensive manufactures,[3] such as tex-

the limited scope for exports of manufacturers from developing to developed countries and states that "long term prospects are for low growth in the latter countries and this will impede any significant reversal of the declines in the terms of trade experienced by the developing countries during the recent past."

[3] See *World Development Report 1984*, p. 43, and James Riedel, "Trade as the Engine of Growth in Developing Countries Revisited," *Economic Journal* 94 (1984), 373. Manufactures today account for 46% of nonfuel exports of the main developing countries, and all (nonfuel) primary exports account for 54% of nonfuel exports. Africa is a region in which dependence on a single primary export has not diminished (*World Development Report 1984*, p. 43).

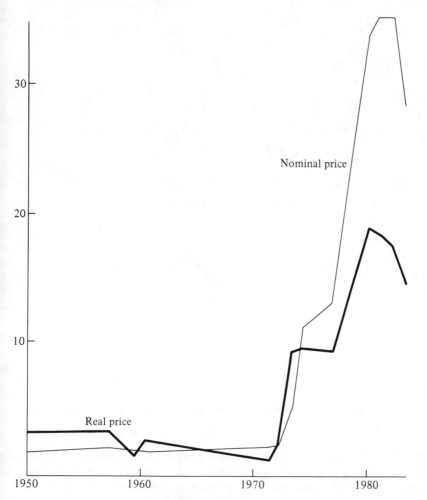

Figure 4.2. Crude oil prices in nominal terms (1970 = 100) and deflated by the U.S. GDP deflator.

tiles, steel, or footwear. It is generally recognized that the export prospects for both categories are not very good.

Primary commodity prices (other than the price of oil) recently reached an all-time low in real terms (see Figures 4.1 and 4.2). They also have a history of extreme volatility, following and often amplifying business cycles, as shown in Figure 4.3. Primary commodities are therefore currently a poor income source, and are in general a very unreliable one.

Exports of labor intensive manufactures are encountering increasing protectionism in industrial-country markets. The multifiber agreement

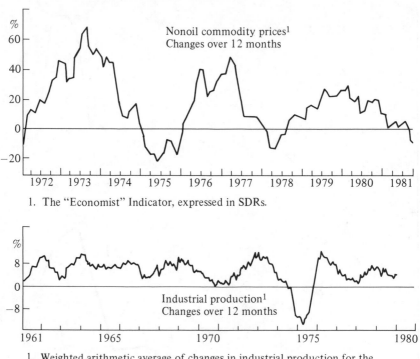

1. The "Economist" Indicator, expressed in SDRs.

1. Weighted arithmetic average of changes in industrial production for the
Group of Ten countries and Switzerland.
Weights are based on gross national products for the year 1975.

Figure 4.3. Commodity price and industrial production cycles, 1961–
81.

provides an effective restriction on textile exports by developing to industrial countries, and the demise of basic steelmaking in Western Europe
and in the United States has led to protection of that industry.[4] Footwear
manufacturers in Europe and the United States are also becoming increasingly vocal about the need for protection, although in that field there
have been fewer protective moves. The prospects for exports of many
labor-intensive products are therefore not very good either. In this context, concerns about the success of export-led policies seem justified.

In fact, even some of the oil-exporting countries, which certainly succeeded in maintaining high prices, did not perform well. Consider, for
example, the middle-income oil-exporting countries in the period 1973–
82. On average these countries grew less than those middle-income coun-

[4] See, for example, Z. A. Silberston, "The Multi-Fibre Agreement and the U.K. Economy,"
Her Majesty's Stationery Office, London, 1984, and Ingo Walter, "Structural Adjustment
and Trade Policy in the International Steel Industry," chap. 14 of *Trade Policy in the
1980's* (W. Cline, ed.), MIT Press, Cambridge, Mass., 1983.

Table 4.1 *Real GNP growth, 1960-82*

Real GNP growth	1960-73	1973-9	1980	1981	1982
Industrial market economies	4.9	2.8	1.3	1.3	-0.5
All developing countries	6.3	5.2	2.5	2.4	1.9
Low income[a]	5.6	4.8	5.9	4.8	5.2
Middle-income oil importers	6.3	5.6	4.3	0.9	0.7
Middle-income oil exporters	6.9	4.9	-2.4	2.4	0.9
High-income oil exporters[b]	10.7	7.7	7.4	0.0	—

[a] Up to $U.S. 390 GNP per capita.
[b] Oman, Libya, Saudia Arabia, Kuwait, United Arab Emirates.
Source: World Bank, *World Development Report* 1984, p. 11.

tries that were oil importers (Table 4.1). The expansion of traditional exports, even under the most propitious international market conditions, is therefore not a reliable source of economic growth.

Why then is there this continued emphasis on expanding traditional exports as the main road to development? Increased exports are sometimes associated with free markets and with the benefits that derive from them. Export-led policies are contrasted with import-substitution policies, or with tariff barriers to trade, both of which policies interfere with free markets and have been widely criticized as leading to inefficiency. Export-led policies are thus seen as closer to free markets than their traditional import-substitution alternatives, and so more likely to reap the benefits of free markets.

This is a plausible argument, but one having little theoretical or empirical basis. Export promotion often requires active government intervention. If an export-promotion policy is followed rather energetically, it may be further removed from the free market than a very mild system of tariffs or restrictions. An expansion in exports that requires wage controls and substantial tax incentives, as has been the case in countries such as Argentina and Brazil in the 1970s, can hardly be seen as one consistent with free markets.

Moreover, those countries that have succeeded in achieving high rates of growth and an expansion of exports have also had rather controlled economies. Examples are South Korea, Japan, and Taiwan. Japan controls its capital markets strongly, practicing industrial policies, import limitation in several sectors, and a careful policy of export targeting.[5] In South Korea, almost all investment is carried out by the government,

[5] See, for example, Gary R. Saxonhouse, "The Micro and Macroeconomics of Foreign Sales to Japan," in *Trade Policy in the 1980's* (op. cit.), p. 259, sections on Tariffs, Non-Tariff Barriers, and Japan's Illiberal Institutions. See also Stephen D. Cohen, *Uneasy Partnership*, Ballinger Publishing Co., Boston, 1985

through a centralized investment planning board.[6] Taiwan provides yet another example of an economy where the evolution of industrial structure is strongly influenced by the government.[7] Success in the promotion of exports therefore appears to be achieved by careful government intervention, rather than by unaided or free markets.

In view of the fact that empirical observation does not support a universal connection between free markets and successful export promotion, we ask whether there are theoretical arguments that might have led to this association. By far the strongest theoretical arguments linking exports and free markets are provided by the neoclassical theory of trade. The main result of this theory is that countries are better off when they trade freely than in complete isolation or autarchy. To achieve these gains from trade, it is required that labor-rich countries export labor-intensive products and capital-rich countries export capital-intensive products. This naturally leads to an international division of labor, each country exporting according to its relative advantage. In this view the relative advantage of the developing countries is their abundant and cheap labor. Poverty is thus their relative advantage.

Neoclassical trade theory only compares complete isolation with free trade, and is mute about the effects of an expansion from current levels of exports. However, whether to trade or to remain in isolation is not the main dilemma facing developing countries today: All countries trade. Rather, their dilemma is whether or not to expand exports, and if so which exports to promote. The question is often the right balance between the domestic sectors and the international sectors of the economy. Such choices are extremely important in countries such as Mexico and Venezuela, which must decide whether or not to use scarce investment resources to develop their oil exports, and Argentina and Brazil, which export labor-intensive grains, beef, and meat by-products (such as leather goods) using resources (such as land) that could be used for production oriented toward domestic markets. The choice is also important to Honduras, Nicaragua, and Ecuador, which must decide how to allocate land for the production of fruit exports (bananas) and the production of local food staples. The choice has also been traditionally important to Cuba, which has used scarce investment resources to specialize very strongly in the production of sugar for exports.

The neoclassical theory of gains from trade provides little guidance on such policy questions. There is no result in this theory predicting that exporting more labor-intensive products is better than exporting fewer. In

[6] L. L. Wade and B. S. Kim, *Economic Development of South Korea*, Praeger Publishers, New York, 1978.
[7] C.-Y. Lin, *Industrialization in Taiwan, 1946–72*. Praeger, New York, 1973.

particular, there is no theorem predicting that the expansion of international demand for labor-intensive products will help those developing countries that expand their exports of such products. Even when economic growth of the industrial region leads it to expand its demand for imports of labor-intensive goods, this may or may not be favorable for the developing countries that export labor-intensive products. Neoclassical theory is mute about these questions.

Although the neoclassical results on gains from trade are powerful, and certainly correct within an appropriate context, it would be too ambitious to expect them to hold in all situations. Neoclassical theory cannot answer questions it was not developed to consider. One such question concerns the effects of increases in the volume of trade. Another relates to trade among widely different regions. Fifty years ago most international trade took place among the industrial nations; today 40% of OECD exports are purchased by developing countries. Fifty years ago we questioned whether or not to trade; now we ask how much to trade and how to balance the international and domestic sectors of our economies.

In this chapter, we present an analysis of export-led strategies based on traditional commodities. This analysis is conducted within a framework appropriate to present-day policy concerns. It indicates the circumstances in which such strategies can be expected to succeed, and those in which they cannot. In the latter case, alternative policies are considered. These take into account not only import substitution, but also more broadly defined development strategies, including such free market alternatives as exporting nontraditional products or trading with less traditional partners. The latter two alternatives appear to be winning a place in international trade statistics: At present the most dynamic segment of the international market is trade among developing countries, namely South–South trade.[8] Within South–South trade, the most dynamic segment is that of exports of engineering products, which are skill- and capital-intensive rather than labor-intensive.[9] Overall, exports of manufactures from developing countries to developing countries are much more capital-intensive than those to industrial countries,[10] further evidence that by trading among themselves some developing countries are beginning to break out of traditional patterns of specialization.

[8] See, for example, "Part II: Economic Cooperation Among Developing Countries," Table 1 of Chap. 1 in *Trade and Development Report,* UNCTAD, 1983, and B. Cizelj and M. Fuks, "Trade Among Developing Countries–Evaluations of Achievements and Potential," *The World Bank, Conference on "South–South Trade or North–South Trade,"* Ljubljana, February 1983. These show that South–South trade is the most dynamic segment of the international economy even when we exclude mineral fuels.

[9] Cizelj and Fuks, *op. cit.*

[10] See O. Havrylyshyn and M. Wolf, "Recent Trends in Trade Among Developing Countries," *European Economic Review* 21, (1983) 333–62.

4.2   Classical trade theory: gains from trade

Before discussing particular policy issues, it seems useful to provide a bird's-eye view of the neoclassical theories of international trade on which export-led recommendations are usually based. Our arguments can then be presented with more clarity and rigor.

Neoclassical trade theory originated in the Heckscher–Ohlin model of the 1930s, which was developed to answer the question: Why do countries trade? This theory provided a rigorous answer by analyzing the welfare effects of trade on the trading economies. The general answer: Trade between countries takes place because the traders benefit from it.

The neoclassical theory had two main kinds of result on the welfare effects of trade: those centered on "gains from trade" and those based on "factor price equalization." These became the pillars on which the theory was constructed. They have been generalized, expanded, and applied very widely, so that their conclusions have reached the noneconomist and acquired the status of conventional wisdom. They are often used to substantiate claims that more trade is better for all, especially when each trading region specializes according to its relative advantage.[11]

It is important to understand the analytical framework from which these results arise. The Heckscher–Ohlin model of international trade is usually presented in the framework of two regions trading with one another in two products. Each region uses two factors of production, labor and capital; one good is more labor-intensive and the other more capital-intensive. The two countries are identical in all respects except for a difference in their factor endowments: One country has more labor and the other more capital. This difference in endowments leads to different product and factor prices in each region before trade takes place.

Each country produces two goods: One is labor-intensive, and the other capital-intensive. In isolation – that is, prior to trade – the labor-intensive product in the labor-rich country has a lower price than the same product in the other country. Factor prices are also different in the two regions. In particular, in isolation the rewards of labor, namely wages, are lower in the country with more labor.

When international trade takes place, the prices of the two traded commodities are equalized in the international market: Each commodity sells for the same price in each of the two regions. The new (world) price of

---

[11] For the limitations of such claims, see P. Samuelson, "The Gains from Trade Once Again," *Economic Journal* 72 (December 1962), 820–9. Samuelson states "Practical men and economic theorists have always known that trade may help some people and hurt others . . . What in the way of policy can we conclude from the fact that trade is a potential boon? Very little."

labor-intensive products is higher than the previous isolation price in the labor-rich country, but lower than the previous isolation price in the capital-rich country. A similar change occurs in the price of the capital-intensive product. Who gains from this change in prices?

Each region exports that commodity that utilizes best its most abundant factor. Thus the labor-rich region exports labor-intensive products, and the capital-rich region, capital-intensive products. A relatively higher price for labor-intensive commodities therefore benefits the labor-rich country, by increasing the value of its exports and lowering the value of its imports. Similarly, the new world prices for capital-intensive goods benefit the capital-rich country. International trade therefore leads to changes in prices that are beneficial to both countries.

For each region, the world price of their speciality item is higher than it was in isolation. Each country can now consume more by specializing in the exports of the good in which it has a "relative advantage" and that has become dearer, while importing the good in which the other has an advantage and that is now less expensive. All these results are generally summarized by the phrase "gains from trade."

A second result links these "gains from trade" with the equalization of factor prices across regions. In isolation, wages are lower in the labor-rich region. It is of interest to know whether wages in the labor-intensive region increase or decrease after trade. If they increase, the gains from trade are also associated with a betterment of the lot of the very poor, the wage-earners in the labor-intensive country.

In the Heckscher–Ohlin model factors of production, labor and capital, are not traded internationally. The price of a factor therefore need not be the same across the two regions. However, there are special conditions under which international trade does lead to the equalization of factor prices across regions. The "factor price equalization" theorem provides conditions under which, after trade, labor is paid the same in the two regions, as is capital. While these conditions are not very general, the result is an important finding. The equalization of factor prices means that wages in the labor-rich country rise to a new world level, at which they are closer to the initial level of wages in the capital-rich country. Under such conditions, we can say that specialization in the production of the labor-intensive good, which is a form of international division of labor, improves the distribution of income within the labor-rich country. More can be said yet.

The relative advantages of the two regions change as factor prices change. When wages in the labor-rich region increase, its relative advantage decreases, since labor-intensive goods are more costly to produce. This theory therefore predicts that relative advantages tend to disappear with continued trade. The factors that lead to the international division of labor are thus expected to disappear with time. It is predicted that the international division of labor will self-destruct. Any inequalities in the roles of the two regions are deemed temporary.

The appeal of these results on gains from trade and factor price equalization has been powerful enough to shape most formalized thinking on the theory of trade and on international economic relations over the past thirty years, and to permeate policy thinking in a pervasive manner. However, the limitations of these results, both empirical and theoretical, are now rather clear.

It is generally acknowledged that the Heckscher–Ohlin model has not provided an adequate explanation for several salient features of the postwar period. In this period, the volume of international trade increased in a historically unprecedented fashion, while wealth differentials and the division of labor between the North and the South became more pronounced. Furthermore, it is generally acknowledged that the distribution of income within the South did not improve during this period.[12] Neither gains from trade nor factor price equalization theories seem consistent with these facts. A concern is often voiced that inequalities, far from disappearing, have become more entrenched. W. Arthur Lewis has recently observed that "the market works to concentrate rather than to diffuse the benefits of trade."[13] Of course, exogenous historical explanations could be invoked for those empirical observations at variance with the theory. However, this would amount to an implicit recognition of the limited explanatory powers of the traditional theory.

Added to these empirical observations, several objections have been raised at the theoretical level. In the classical theory, the two trading region are identical in all respects except for factor endowments. This feature is unrealistic in today's world economy in which much of the world's trade is transacted between industrial and developing countries, with striking contrasts between the economies of these two groups of countries.

It should be noted, however, that the Heckscher–Ohlin theory was not designed to explain North–South trade, but rather to explain trade

[12] The shares of resources and expenditures of developed and under developed countries became more unequal from 1960 to 1972. See P. Streeten and S. J. Burki, "Basic Needs, Some Issues," *World Development Report 1978*, Fig. 9, chap. 5. The income distribution within many third-world countries also worsened, and considerable evidence suggests that the incomes of the bottom 10%–20% have fallen in absolute terms in the past twenty-five years; see Mabub ul Haq, Annex 2, in J. Tinbergen et al., *RIO: Reshaping the International Order*, E. P. Dutton, New York, 1978.

[13] W. A. Lewis, "Development Economics in the '80s," Seminar Paper, Princeton University, February 1983; *American Economic Association Papers and Proceedings*, 1984.

among regions of similar economic characteristics, such as industrial countries trading with each other. Over the postwar period as a whole, North–North trade comprised the great majority of all international trade. It is only recently that North–South trade has become sizable: 40% of OECD exports are now sold to developing countries. The structure of international trade has thus changed considerably since Heckscher and Ohlin proposed their model of international trade, and this requires a corresponding change in our analytical tools.

4.3   The North–South model: structural differences between the traders

As a move in this direction, we shall consider a model that is consistent with perfectly competitive markets and flexible prices throughout, but that allows for differences in economic structures between the trading regions.[14] When these differences are small, one obtains results in the spirit of Heckscher–Ohlin. However, if the economic structures are significantly different, different results emerge and, in particular, one can describe precisely when the expansion of trade is beneficial to the South and when it is not.

Two types of structural difference between the regions are considered:

1. *Differences in technologies:* The degree of technological diversity between the traditional and the industrial sectors in the South is generally much larger than in the North.

2. *Differences in the behavior of labor and capital markets:* Labor supply in the South is highly responsive to changes in real wages, due, for example, to a significant migration from the subsistence to industrial sectors of the economy. Labor supply in the North is less responsive to changes in the real wage. Capital supply in the North is responsive to the rate of return on capital; capital supply in the South is less responsive.

---

[14] This theory was developed between 1977 and 1982 as part of a UNITAR research project conducted by G. Chichilnisky at Harvard University, Columbia University, and the University of Essex. The main publications are "Terms of Trade and Domestic Distribution: Export-Led Growth with Abundant Labor," *Journal of Development Economics* 8(2) (1981), 163–92; "Basic Goods, Commodity Transfers and the International Economic Order," *Journal of Development Economics* 7(4)(1980), 505–19; "The Transfer Problem with Three Agents Once Again: Characterization, Uniqueness and Stability," *Journal of Development Economics* 13(1–2) (1983) 237–48; "North–South Trade and Export-Led Strategies," *Journal of Development Economics* (1984); "Terms of Trade and Domestic Distribution: A Rejoinder to Rejoinders," *Journal of Development Economics,* 15 (1984), 177–84, and "A General Equilibrium Theory of North–South Trade," chap. 1 in *Essays in the Honor of K. J. Arrow,* W. Heller, D. Starrett, and R. Starr (eds.), Cambridge University Press, 1986.

Empirical studies of these two structural characteristics for a number of developing and industrial countries confirm that there are indeed important differences in these respects.[15]

These two structural differences taken together, or indeed just the greater dualism of technologies in the South together with an assumption that wages are spent mostly on the labor-intensive goods, lead to important general equilibrium effects. We use the term "general equilibrium" to indicate a simultaneous consideration of supply and demand across several markets linked together by market clearing conditions. Our next task is to analyze these effects.

One can give precise conditions under which increasing the exports of labor-intensive products leads to an improvement in terms of trade, real wages, and consumption in the South. Equally, outside those conditions, an expansion of exports leads to worse terms of trade and export revenues, to lower real wages, and to a deterioration of the distribution of income in the South. These negative effects from an export expansion usually occur when technologies are very different in the traditional and the industrial sectors, a phenomenon we call "technological dualism," and when labor is very abundant. Even when labor is not very abundant, the same results obtain when the South exports labor-intensive goods and most of its wage income is spent on such goods.

Such negative outcomes from increasing exports are not surprising: They are quite consistent with observations made over the years about the consequences of export-led strategies in many Latin American, African, and Asian countries. Indeed, empirical studies of Argentina's exports of meat and meat by-products, of Mexico's exports of oil, and of Sri Lanka's exports of tea support these theoretical findings.[16] Figure 4.4 depicts movements in oil export levels and oil prices for Mexico, which for certain periods confirm the negative connection between export expansion and terms of trade. There are also other empirical studies of India and of Brazil[17] that were concerned with the expansion of export crops in the face

[15] The North–South model discussed here has been subject to empirical testing. This included econometric tests of trade between Sri Lanka and the United Kingdom, which confirmed the basic structure of the model and in particular substantiated the possibility that an expansion of trade in labor-intensive products may have harmful effects. See G. Chichilnisky, G. M. Heal, and J. Podivinsky, "Trade Between Sri Lanka and the U.K.: An Econometric Study of North–South Trade," Working Paper, Columbia Business School, 1982. Other empirical studies of the model include World Bank studies on Argentina and Mexico; see G. Chichilnisky and D. McLeod, "Agricultural Productivity and Trade: Argentina and the U.S.A.," World Bank, Working Paper No. 1984-4, Division of Global Analysis and Projections, and G. Chichilnisky, G. Heal, and D. McLeod, "Resources Trade and Debt: Mexico and the U.S.A.," World Bank, Working Paper No. 1984-5, Division of Global Analysis and Projections.

[16] See footnote 15.

[17] See, for example, A. K. Sen, *Famines,* Oxford University Press, London, 1981 on India and D. Alves, "Brazilian Agriculture Export Promotion versus Nutrition," IPE USP, presented at the Development Conference, Yale Growth Center, New Haven, 1978.

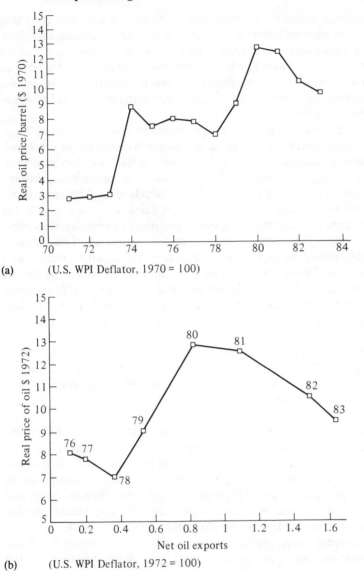

(a)   (U.S. WPI Deflator, 1970 = 100)

(b)   (U.S. WPI Deflator, 1972 = 100)

Figure 4.4. Mexican oil exports and terms of trade, 1960–82: (a) real Mexican oil export price; (b) Mexican oil prices and exports (millions of barrels/day).

of diminished domestic consumption of food and analyzed the same negative correlation between exports and domestic consumption. The evidence is therefore substantial that export-led strategies can lead to domestic hardship. Indeed, IMF recommendations of export-led policies are often associated with recommendations of austerity measures and salary repression, suggesting a view consistent with the empirical observations reported here.[18]

The reader may be puzzled by the apparent contrast between these empirical findings and the supporting theoretical results on the one hand, and the predictions of the neoclassical theory on the other. Since neoclassical trade theory in all its generality has never been substantiated empirically, we must pose this question at a theoretical level: Is there any contradiction between the neoclassical results on gains from trade and factor price equalization, and these negative outcomes of export-led strategies? If so, how does the contradiction emerge? A second set of questions is empirical: How do we explain the success stories of Japan, Germany, and more recently Taiwan, Korea, and Singapore, all of which thrived on export-led policies? Is there any rhyme or reason in this highly complex issue? Can we explain why certain countries succeed and others fail when following export-led strategies? When export-led strategies fail, can we offer palatable, realistic alternatives?

The rest of this chapter will show that there is no contradiction between the neoclassical theory and the negative results on export-led policies reported above.[19] In the process we shall also explain why certain countries fail and others succeed with export-led policies, and suggest alternatives.

The key to our results lies in the questions which we ask: Asking the right questions is usually the most important step in research. The neoclassical theory asks whether trade is better than autarchy or complete isolation. This, to us, is an important question but one that is almost irrelevant in today's world. Of course trade is better than no trade, and because of this all countries trade. The question we ask is, instead, whether from the present situation we would gain by *expanding* trade.

This latter question is at the core of an evaluation of export-led strategies. It requires that we compare two market equilibria, one with less and the other with more trade. However, the neoclassical theory compares a free trade equilibrium with a particular *disequilibrium* position, one involving no international trade at all. A move from disequilibrium (isolation) to equilibrium (trade) improves welfare, since, as we saw in Chapter 3, competitive market equilibria are Pareto-efficient. However, nothing

[18] See, e.g., footnote 1.
[19] See also footnote 11.

in the neoclassical theory predicts what happens to the welfare of the traders as the world moves from one market equilibrium to the next, the latter one having more trade between the countries. This is because, for such moves to occur, a change must take place elsewhere – a change of a type that is not considered in the neoclassical models but is considered here. Such a change could be in the so-called "exogenous parameters" of the model: in preferences or demands, in factor supplies, or in technologies. We concentrate here on changes in such underlying parameters that lead to a new state of the world economy in which the South exports more. The underlying parameters shift and a new equilibrium emerges, one with more trade. Prices change, and with them supplies, final consumption, exports, imports, and the distribution of income within and across countries. This is the nature of our experiment, quite different from that underlying the classical question of to trade or not to trade.

Now, the reader may ask: How do these underlying exogenous parameters shift? The answer is quite general: Any cause is acceptable. It could be government policy affecting final demand for products, or an exogenous shift of consumer preferences leading to changes in demand. As long as trade volume increases (following the parameters' shift), we are able to study the impact of increasing exports on prices and welfare. This is explained in more detail in Chapter 11, which describes the North–South model.

In addition to asking different questions, there are two further deviations of our model from the neoclassical framework, deviations that were already pointed out: (1) technologies are generally different in the two regions, and (2) factor supplies change with prices. The latter occurs in different ways in the two regions: Labor supply is typically more responsive to wages in the South; capital supplies are more responsive to the rate of return in the North. In contrast, the Heckscher–Ohlin model is usually formulated with the same technologies in the two trading regions and with a fixed endowment of factors in each of the two regions.

The notion of abundance of labor bears some elaboration. In the Heckscher–Ohlin context being labor-rich means possessing a large, albeit fixed, supply of labor, all of which is employed in equilibrium. In our context, abundant labor means that the labor supply is very responsive to increases in real wages. In a market equilibrium, labor supply and demand still meet at the going wage, but there may be a great deal of extra labor that would be offered at a slightly higher wage. There is an illustrious example in the literature that approximates this concept of labor abundance. This is W. Arthur Lewis's model of economic development, where labor supply is infinitely elastic so that any amount of labor is available at the subsistence wage. Wages, in Lewis's model, are pegged to the subsistence level. The level of employment is determined by demand, and there is typically surplus labor. The present North–South model has a related, albeit different, structure: In this model, labor is abundant in the sense of being very responsive to wages, but is not necessarily in infinitely elastic supply. Wages may, and do, vary.

The model that we use is an instance of the more general Arrow–Debreu model, which is the standard formalization of a competitive market economy.[20] It contains the Heckscher–Ohlin model as a special case: the case when technologies are equal in the two regions and when factor endowments are fixed in both regions. Our model is therefore an evolution from the neoclassical tradition that allows us to deal with present-day concerns such as North–South trade.

We now return to export policies within our two-region, two-commodity, two-factor model.

4.4   The effects of an export expansion

The framework just outlined makes it possible to identify simple conditions on the domestic economy that determine the effects of exporting more labor-intensive goods. The data of the country, as reflected in the sign of one algebraic expression, establish whether higher export levels are associated with better or worse terms of trade, wages, and employment. Typically, abundant labor and dual technologies (conditions that can be quantified and measured) lead to negative outcomes: In such a case exporting more leads to lower terms of trade, lower real wages, and lower employment.

This increase in exports could be initiated by any one of many different causes and still lead to the same results. Among the causes that have been explored are the following:

1. A rise in demand for the labor-intensive exports of the South caused by an economic expansion in the North.
2. A relaxation (rise) in the import quotas that the North has imposed on labor-intensive products imported from the South (such as textiles, footwear, coffee, or jute).
3. An exogenous drop in demand within the South for its export good, leading to an increase in the volume of its exports. This could be initiated by government policies such as tax incentives or domestic consumption quotas.

The last two cases refer to the effects of a government policy. The results

---

[20] See, for example, G. Chichilnisky, "A General Equilibrium Theory of North–South Trade," chap. 1 in *Essays in Honor of Kenneth Arrow* (op. cit.).

results in those cases arise from the interplay between a government policy and the market's responses to this policy. The first case, however, depicts a competitive economy's adjustment to changes in an exogenous parameter of the model. No government policies are involved.

Cases 1 and 2 are perhaps the most surprising. They run counter to a strong but unsubstantiated belief that an industrial expansion of the North must benefit the South if it leads the North to purchase more labor-intensive exports from the South.[21] This belief is often incorrect: An expansion of the North need not benefit the South in any way, even if this leads to more exports from the South. W. Arthur Lewis has argued that the North may not be an adequate "engine of growth" for the South[22] and the statistical evidence of recent years confirms this.[23]

The failure of the North to act as an engine of growth for the South can occur in one of two ways. One is relatively standard. The North's expansion may *not* lead it to import more from the South: Both the exports of the South and their prices may drop as the North's expands. This happens when expansion shifts the North's demand toward the industrial sector and away from the basic sector. The demand for basics drops, together with their relative price. This harms the South as its exports drop and so do their prices.

Alternatively, and this may be more surprising, even if an expansion in the North leads it to import more from the South, the consequences for the South may be negative.[24] In such cases, the South exports more to the North and yet its terms of trade, wages, domestic employment, and consumption all decrease. The North imports more at lower prices and is better off as it consumes more in both sectors of the economy. How does this happen?

The link we seek is between the North's demand for the exports of the South and the South's terms of trade, real wages, and consumption. That

---

[21] A typical expression of this belief is in the *World Development Report 1978* (p. 13): "Since the industrialized countries' demand for imports depends on their income, their economic growth is very important to the export and growth prospects of developing countries."

[22] See W. A. Lewis, "The Evolution of the International Order," Princeton University Press, 1979 and, more recently; Box 3.2 of "Trade as an Engine of Growth," in the *World Development Report 1984*, p. 43; also J. Riedel, "Trade as the Engine of Growth in Developing Countries, Revisited," the *Economic Journal*, 94 (373) (March 1984), 56–73.

[23] For instance, the *World Development Report 1984*, p. 43, states: "The experience of the 1960's and 1970's bears this out. There has been no stable statistical relation between the volume of developing country exports and real income in developed countries in the 1960's and 1970's. Developing countries' exports are not mechanically linked to the growth and level of prosperity in advanced countries."

[24] A full technical derivation of these results is given in G. Chichilnisky, "Terms of Trade and Domestic Distribution: Export-Led Growth with Abundant Labor" (op. cit.) and "North–South Trade and Export-Led Policies" (op. cit.).

this link can be negative is explained clearly and in intuitive terms by K. J. Arrow's comment on the North–South model[25]:

Very loosely, the argument is the following. Suppose the rise in export demand for the (labour-intensive) B commodity were followed by an increase in its price. Since its production is highly labour-intensive, there should be a rise in real wages and, since labour supply is highly responsive to the real wage, a considerable increase in labour supply. The rise in both real wage and labour supply increases even more rapidly the domestic demand for the B commodity, since it is all directed to the B commodity. Hence supply available for export would *decrease,* and therefore would not match the increased demand for exports. It follows that the only way the export demand could be met, under these conditions, would be a *decrease* in the price of commodity B and of real wages.

This argument shows how an increase in the North's demand leads to more exports from the South, but also to lower prices, real wages, and domestic consumption in the South. The reasoning emphasizes the strength of linkages between factor and goods markets in the South and seems worth developing.

An increase in the price of B leads to an increase in both employment and real wages in the South. Wage income thus increases, and so does domestic demand for B. If this demand response is strong, it will thwart any attempt to increase exports. Even as supplies of basics increase, domestic demand for them increases even more, so that less is available for exports. This could happen in a region where there is initially an unsatisfied demand for the basic good, as when there is inadequate consumption of food. As income expands, the demand for food will increase rapidly. Under these conditions, increases in the price of basics lead to lower exports; exports of basics can therefore only increase if there is a drop in their price. This leads in turn to lower real wages, since basics are labor-intensive, and to lower domestic output and consumption.

There is yet another way of seeing this. Under the conditions specified, an increase in the production of exportables leads to more wage income and so to an increase in domestic demand for exportable goods that exceeds the supply increase. Thus, if domestic production increases, exports must drop. Equivalently, the only way exports can increase is if domestic production drops. This leads to lower domestic consumption and allows for more exports. Not a happy situation: one where in order to export more the country must produce and consume less.

It may appear from the above that the responsible element in all this is the strong demand response in the South, and that if this response could be controlled, the problem might disappear. Attempts in this direction are

---

[25] K. J. Arrow, Evaluation of UNITAR Project, "Technology, Domestic Distribution and North–South Relations," UNITAR, U.N. Publications, New York, August 1981.

often made and take the form either of laws limiting the consumption of export goods, as has occurred with beef in Argentina, or of wage repression, as recently in Brazil. However, such measures may not solve the problem. Even when the demand response is not very strong, a similar result emerges when there is a sluggish response of supply to prices. In either case, exports can only increase when employment, wages, production, and domestic consumption all fall. One can hardly advise an increase in exports under these circumstances.

Although Arrow's quote refers to the case of dualism and abundant labor, the same argument applies with dualism alone when most wage income in the South is spent on the labor-intensive export commodity. In such cases, the increase in export demand can only be met when there is a decrease in real wages in the South and in the price of basics. Once again, lower wages are needed to control domestic consumption and to allow increased exports. Lower real wages are, of course, associated with a lower price of the (labor-intensive) basic good.

This dismal outcome of export-led policies is quite consistent with the fact that some international agencies simultaneously require decreased domestic consumption and export expansion by developing countries. In the agencies' viewpoints, these two outcomes are clearly linked.[26]

What about successful export-led policies? Can this theory explain how export promotion can lead to better wages and to an expansion in domestic consumption? The theory can, in fact, explain both the successes and the failures of export-led policies and point out when one of these outcomes is more likely than the other. The sign of one equation predicts whether the effect of an expansion in exports is harmful or beneficial.

As can be expected, there are no blanket statements: Rather one shows that different conditions lead to different results. In other words, different structural characteristics of an economy indicate the need for different policies. Export-led policies lead to positive results when the production system is more homogeneous and when labor supply is less responsive to real wages. An expansion of exports can then lead to attractive outcomes: an improvement in the South's terms of trade and export revenues, increases in domestic employment, in domestic consumption, and in real wages. From an economic viewpoint, therefore, the economic parameters

---

[26] See, for example, J. de Larosière, "Does the Fund Impose Austerity?" (*op. cit.*). Other authors have expressed doubts about IMF prescriptions. W. A. Lewis observes: "The official doctors, the I.M.F., have a standard prescription: clear the markets, look outwards, and balance the budget. This comes from our famous forefather of 1776. It is a palliative rather than a cure, judging by the frequency with which the same patients return." In "Development Economics in the 1980s," Seminar Paper, Princeton University, 1983, published as "The State of Development Theory," *American Economic Review* 74(1) (1984), 1–10.

of dualism and of labor abundance must be considered and, if necessary, modified, before embarking on an export-led policy.

It is worth noting that an expansion of capital-intensive exports may work even when an expansion of labor-intensive exports does not. For this reason, less traditional exports or exports to less traditional partners are often more successful for dual economies with abundant labor: Exports to other developing countries are frequently more capital-intensive than exports to the industrial countries.[27]

4.5   Dual economies and the international division of labor

It is of interest that in dual economies with abundant labor the international division of labor tends to be *reinforced* by the expansion of international trade in labor-intensive products. This is because in this case an increase in exports leads to lower wages in the South, thus reinforcing its relative advantage in labor-intensive products.

This type of relative advantage, derived from poverty, is of course quite different from the advantage derived from productive and well-paid labor. With high labor productivity, total costs can be low even when individual wages are high. Our results indicate that such relative advantages are a better basis for export policies than those derived from mass poverty. The Federal Republic of Germany in the 1960s and Japan, Korea, and Taiwan up to the present are examples of successful exporters with relatively skilled and well-paid labor. Latin American economies, on the other hand, have typically relied on the first type of relative advantages: mass poverty. Their export policies have on the whole had rather poor outcomes.[28]

A further point is that, in dual economies with abundant labor, the expansion of trade does not equalize factor prices across regions. Factor prices may actually drift further apart as trade expands, a fact that is

[27] In 1977, the capital/labor ratios for NIC (newly industrialized country) exports were as follows. For their primary exports to developing countries, $53,589 per worker; for their primary exports to developed countries, $15,075 per worker. *Source:* Table 10, p. 355 of Oli Havrylyshyn and Martin Wolf, "Recent Trends in Trade Among Developing Countries," *European Economic Review* 21 (1983), 333–62.

[28] Cases in point have been Argentina and Chile during the period 1970–82 in which they pursued aggressive export promotion, free market policies, and wage repression. Argentina grew at 1.5% and Chile at 1.9% over this period, a significant drop from the levels 4.3% and 4.4%, respectively, over the previous decade 1960–70. For Mexico the 1970–82 GDP growth rate was 6.4%, 1.3% less than the previous 1960–70 period, while the country became one of the major oil exporters. Venezuela grew at 4.1% during 1970–82 while becoming a major oil exporter, whereas its 1960–70 growth rate was significantly higher, at 6.0%. For growth rates, see *World Development Report 1984*, pp. 220–1. Overall, Latin American countries increased their exports by 24.1% in the period 1970–80; see UNCTAD *Trade and Development Report*, 1983, Table 1, chap. II.

consistent with history. The expansion of trade in the postwar period did not decrease wealth differentials between workers in the industrial countries and those in the developing countries.[29]

It is worth noting that in a model with different technologies in the two regions, the prices of factors are generally different in the two regions at the market equilibrium. This happens in both a Heckscher–Ohlin model with different technologies, and in the North–South model. However, in the classical model, factor prices in the South will often move *toward* those of the North as the countries move from autarchy to free trade, leading to an increase in wages in the South. It has been inferred from this that an increase in trade will always improve the distribution of income in the South, though this inference certainly does not follow without additional assumptions. If the South has abundant labor and dual technologies, a case not included in the Heckscher–Ohlin model, it can be established that an increase in the volume of trade will actually worsen the distribution of income in the South.

4.6   Export enclaves and natural resources

It has already been indicated that the negative outcomes from an export expansion occur in two distinct but related cases: One is where the South is characterized by dualism and abundant labor, and the other where the South is dualistic and exports a "wage good," namely a good on which most wage income is spent. Examples are agricultural goods and manufactured products that are consumed domestically from wage income, such as meat or meat by-products in Argentina, jute and textiles in India and Pakistan, or rice in Thailand.

The analysis is also valid in a third case, which represents a considerable generalization of these: the case where the region exports a labor-intensive product that is produced almost exclusively for export. Examples are coffee and soya beans in Brazil, bananas in Central America, and tea in Sri Lanka. In this case, we consider a model with three rather than two goods in the South: an industrial good, a so-called basic good, and the labor-intensive export. This export good is called an "enclave" because its domestic content is relatively small and it is not used as a main input to production in other domestic industries. The enclave is disassociated from the domestic economy both on the supply and the demand sides.[30]

The results are very similar in this third case. With abundant labor and dual technologies, an increase in exports of an enclave good also leads to

---

[29] See footnote 12.
[30] For full details see G. Chichilnisky, "North–South Trade with Export Enclaves," Working Paper, Columbia University, 1983.

lower terms of trade and to a decrease in domestic consumption of basics. This can also be traced to linkages between factor and goods markets, but of a different nature, since the enclave good is not consumed domestically. It results from the competition for the use of factors between the enclave and the domestically consumed basic good. The competition arises because both the enclave and the basic good are labor-intensive.[31]

At an empirical level, this suggests a negative relationship between the domestic consumption of basic goods and the exports of a labor-intensive enclave. This is certainly consistent with the findings of various authors, who have noted in several studies[32] that regions suffering from acute food shortages may actually be achieving record levels of exports of food. So the domestic shortages in these cases do not arise from the lack of food supplies: They arise rather from the way in which the market allocates the available food resources.

The level of food consumption, which measures the extent to which a main basic need is satisfied, is not determined by food supply per capita, but rather by the outcome of a complex set of market forces. Famine and underconsumption may in some cases result not from population explosion or supply shortfalls, but from the workings of the market.

Perfectly competitive markets, which lead to economic efficiency, may also lead to hunger and starvation in the face of plenty. The very market forces that lead to an efficient allocation of goods and services may also lead to insufficient food consumption by some, as exports expand. That this occurs with dual technologies and abundant labor, and not with homogeneous technologies and abundant capital, is both a warning and a basis from which to rethink export strategies.

We note finally that the same kind of analysis can be extended to cover cases where the export commodity is a mineral resource that is extracted primarily for sale to the international market and is not labor-intensive. Examples are copper in Chile or Zaïre, oil in Mexico or Venezuela, and bauxite in Guyana. The results that emerge from the analysis of such cases again show a relationship between the success of export promotion and the characteristics of the exporting economy such as demands and technologies. These are described in detail in Chapter 7 on resources and North–South trade.

---

[31] The mechanism that drives the results is as follows: As wages increase there is a higher demand for basics. This leads, in turn, to more employment in the basic sector. Even though total labor supply increases, less labor is employed in the enclave and production decreases. Higher wages thus lead to lower exports of the enclave good. It follows that a drop in wages and domestic consumption is required in order to increase exports.

[32] See footnote 17.

4.7 Evaluation of export policies: Is poverty a relative advantage?

This section discusses the conditions that are necessary for a country to reap the potential benefits from increased exports, and analyzes cases where export-oriented policies have been successful. Alternative policies are suggested when such conditions are not satisfied.

In general terms it can be said that sustained growth of the South cannot be based on the relative advantage of cheap labor associated with mass poverty. To the extent that widespread poverty is consistent with abundant labor supply and leads to dual technologies (technologies in the industrial sector that are very different from those in the rest of the economy), export-led policies may lead to a deterioration of the terms of trade of the South, lower wages, and eventually lower export revenues. Even though in the short run the revenues accruing to a small elite could be increased, in the medium and in the long run the country as a whole will be worse off. This possibility has been substantiated by econometric studies of trade between selected industrial and developing countries.[33]

At this stage it seems appropriate to discuss the conditions necessary to reap the potential benefits from an expansion of exports. A first requirement is that productivity in the traditional sectors, such as agriculture, be increased. W. A. Lewis sees this as a prerequisite for industrialization and for better terms of trade for the developing countries.[34] Our analysis leads to similar conclusions.[35] Such increases in productivity are consistent with a better distribution of income and may also lead to lower rates of population growth and thus to less labor abundance. When accompanied by more homogeneous technologies, these are propitious conditions for positive outcomes from an export expansion.

Measures that only protect local production and neglect demand effects, such as generalized import substitution and infant industry protection, are not always successful substitutes for export promotion and may lead to serious inefficiencies. Such policies deal only with the supply side of the market; the impact on domestic demand is neglected. A typical example of such failure was the strong protection and subsidization of the automobile industry in Chile and Argentina in the 1950s and 1960s, which led to more domestic production than could be absorbed. Not enough wealth existed to support domestic consumption of the large quantities of automobiles that were produced under these subsidized conditions. The outcome was bankruptcy and the closing down of many

---

[33] See footnote 15.
[34] See W. A. Lewis, *The Evolution of the International Order* (op. cit.).
[35] See G. Chichilnisky and D. McLeod, "Agricultural Productivity and Trade: Argentina and the U.S." (op. cit.).

automobile factories, which led to an unemployment crisis with deep social consequences in regions such as Cordoba, Argentina.

What is required is an appreciation of the two sides of the market simultaneously, of both demand and supply. It must be realized that local populations count in both sides of the profit equation, that is, as customers as well as factors of production. This requires the development of the domestic market as a whole, which in turn requires increases in the productivity of the traditional or the rural sectors.

Examples of successful export-led policies in the past twenty years, which were widely discussed in the 1970s, include Japan, the Federal Republic of Germany, and more recently Korea, Taiwan, and Singapore. In each case domestic markets were strong. In Taiwan and Korea agricultural productivity had grown at an extremely high rate since the 1950s, essentially due to successful land reform policies.[36] Employment, wages, and domestic consumption in these successful export-oriented countries were all relatively high.[37] By contrast, the less successful export promotion policies pursued by Latin American countries were built on dual economies with "abundant" and very cheap labor, as in Brazil in the 1970s, and often accompanied by a depressed domestic market as in the case of Argentina and Chile during the 1970s. Agricultural productivity in the latter two countries has been stagnant or even declining.[38]

Latin America's export-led policies relied largely on cheap labor provided by mass poverty: Their success was often predicated on the government's ability to repress real wages. In the case of Argentina, this was often coupled with a moratorium on domestic consumption of the export good, meat, to allow for increased exports. This is consistent with our observation that in many cases domestic consumption must drop before exports can expand. What is needed is precisely the opposite: an export expansion that leads to better wages and to a domestic expansion. It is obvious that an increase in exports is only desirable if it is associated with more, rather than less, domestic welfare.

[36] From 1949 to 1953 Taiwan launched a major program of land reform. A land bank was established to provide easy credit terms to tenant farmers. The government made it possible for eight out of ten households to own their own farms, compared to three out of ten before the war. Between 1950 and 1970 farm production expanded three times more rapidly than the historical growth trend, with very high increases in annual rate growth of real wages. Between 1958 and 1968 the annual growth of real wages of the agricultural sector was 3.4% and rose to 7.9% between 1968 and 1978, according to *Taiwan Statistical Data Book 1981*, Council for Economic Planning and Development, Taiwan.

[37] See *Major Statistics of Korean Economy 1982*, Economic Planning Board, Korea, and *Taiwan Statistical Data Book 1981* (op. cit.).

[38] By 1980–82, the average index of food production per capita for Korea had risen from 1969–71 = 100 to 125. This increase exceeds those in Chile (98), Mexico (104), Argentina (122), Uruguay (109), and Venezuela (95), all of which are upper-middle-income countries. Indeed, Chile and Venezuela both showed a drop in per capita food production over this period. (Source: World Bank, *World Development Report 1984*, p. 229.)

Most policy makers in Latin American perceive that export success depends on the ability to repress wages: This would lower the costs of labor-intensive products. It would also decrease domestic demand and thus liberate a large part of domestic production for export. This perception arises from a misunderstanding and leads to great economic strains and eventually to failure of the policy.

Although export policies based on cheap labor and lower domestic consumption have in the short run led to more exports, very often they have also led in the medium run to lower terms of trade, domestic recession, and ballooning international debt. Export policies that produce a serious deterioration in the distribution of income also lead to economic instability: capital outflow, increasing import bills, and trade deficits. Brazil in the late 1970s and early 1980s is one example of such an export-led policy gone sour; Mexico in the late 1970s and Argentina in the 1970s are two more. These countries would have been better placed to export if:

1. their labor were more productive and thus better paid, especially in the traditional sectors;
2. they had ceased to attempt to increase exports of labor-intensive products and raw materials and instead had developed their export markets for more capital-intensive products, perhaps to other developing countries; and
3. they had reached a more balanced policy between production for domestic consumption and for exports.

None of these conditions requires either import substitution or a violation of market freedom. They require, rather, a shrewd marketing strategy and a commitment to increased productivity and to basic human dignity.

The conditions suggested here were indeed satisfied in the countries that succeeded in their export-led strategies: Japan, Germany (FRG), Korea, and Taiwan. Their export strategies were based on highly skilled labor that was, on the whole, much better paid than it was in Latin America. As already pointed out, these countries also had highly productive agricultural sectors. None of these successful exporters remained long as exporters of raw materials or as exporters of very labor-intensive products.

4.8 North–South wealth differentials and the income distribution in the south

The distribution of wealth between the North and the South has been a matter of continued international concern. The distribution of wealth within the South is often seen as a separate phenomenon, to the point that one hears calls for the South to "put its house in order first" as a response to the moral imperative to decrease North – South wealth differentials.

However, these two phenomena are not independent. We saw that the North – South terms of trade are related to the distribution of income within the South. These terms of trade are indeed also related to the distribution of income within the North. Since domestic and international distributions are related, it may in fact be impossible for the South to put its house in order first: Improvement of the distribution within the South may require a prior or simultaneous improvement of North – South economic relations.

As is often the case in economics, causal relations cannot be established easily. However, better terms of trade with the North are indeed associated with a better distribution of income in the South. Conversely, lower terms of trade for the South lead to worse distributions within the South. The international market is therefore an important factor in shaping the domestic distribution of income within this region. At the same time the impact of international markets on one particular economy depends on the prevailing market and technological conditions *within* that economy.

The relationships between domestic and international variables are complex and pervasive, and cannot be neglected. Even variables that are usually considered domestic, such as the distribution of income, are interdependent across regions. Indeed, they are mediated by the international market. It is therefore of great import to develop consistent domestic and international policies. This requires conceptual frameworks that are appropriate to our evolving international economy.

CHAPTER 5

Armaments and North–South trade

5.1 International trade in armaments

International flows of armaments have become increasingly commercialized. Consider the United States, one of the largest arms producers in the world. In the period 1974–83, the United States shifted from providing arms mostly as military assistance to exporting on commercial terms, as shown in Table 5.1 and Figures 5.1 and 5.2. This trend continues at present.

Arms flows are increasingly being transacted through the market, rather than being part of a political process. This chapter examines trade in armaments, from the economic point of view, as an important sector of the international market.

5.2 North–South trade in armaments

The most rapidly growing segment of the international market in armaments has been trade between the North and the South. As a matter of fact, armaments trade has shifted dramatically to become almost exclusively a North–South trade. In 1963, the North exported 97% of all armaments traded; of this, 50% was purchased by other countries in the North. These proportions changed strikingly in the past two decades: In 1982, the North still exported a very large fraction of armaments traded, 87%, but now 82% of these exports were purchased by the South. The trade in armaments is currently overwhelmingly a North–South phenomenon: The North exports almost all arms traded and the South imports most of them. Figure 5.3 shows the development of North's and South's participation in the international market in armaments: The underlying data are in Table 5.2.

Table 5.3 shows the absolute increases in arms imports and exports in the North and in the South. In the decade 1963–73, the North's exports increased 98% and its imports decreased 36%. In the same period the South's imports increased 229%. The period 1972–82 replicates this pattern. It is also of interest that in the two periods, the South increased its

Table 5.1. *U.S. military assistance program as compared with commercial exports licensed under the Arms Export Control Act, fiscal years 1974–83*

Fiscal year	Military assistance program[a]	Commercial exports[b]
1974	1,831,808	502,166
1975	1,807,993	546,551
1976	364,041	1,401,999
1977	108,722	1,523,403
1978	220,347	1,676,007
1979	168,255	1,526,992
1980	435,692	1,968,327
1981	313,158	2,198,309
1982[c]	426,305	1,791,248
1983[c]	179,314	2,084,804

[a] The dollar amount worldwide of material and services, other than training programmed for a particular foreign country for which the U.S. government receives no dollar reimbursement in any fiscal year.
[b] The total (worldwide) dollar value of deliveries made against purchases of munitions-controlled items *by foreign governments directly from U.S. manufacturers.* These data are compiled by the Office of Munitions Control, Department of State from manufacturers' export licenses.
[c] Estimated.
Source: Department of Defense, Security Assistance Agency; "Foreign Military Construction Sales & Military Assistance" (1974–83 data from Tables on Military Assistance Program and Commercial Exports).

own exports by a significant proportion; this is in part explained by the low base from which their market participation started. Yet the data show that trade in armaments is overwhelmingly a North–South phenomenon, and the trend is for this North–South pattern to continue.

5.3   Major armament exports and the concentration of the export market

Table 5.4 provides the percentage of total exports originating in major exporting countries over the past twenty years. The concentration in this market is very large, exceeding, for instance, that in the international market for oil. Major exporters are consistently the United States, United Kingdom, France, and the Soviet Union. Together, these four exporters account for about 90% of exports over the past twenty years.

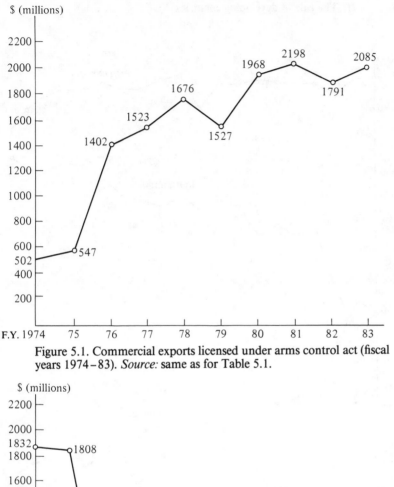

Figure 5.1. Commercial exports licensed under arms control act (fiscal years 1974–83). *Source:* same as for Table 5.1.

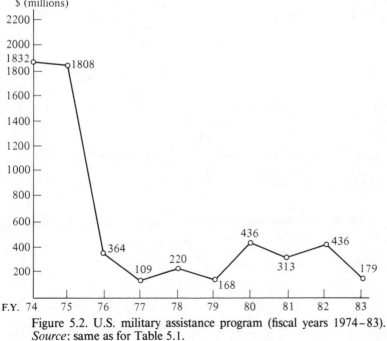

Figure 5.2. U.S. military assistance program (fiscal years 1974–83). *Source*: same as for Table 5.1.

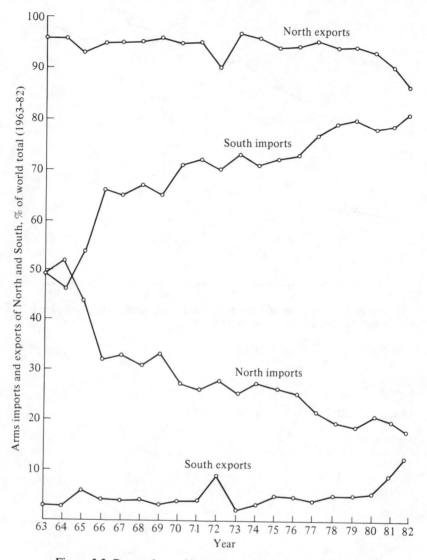

Figure 5.3. Proportions of imports and exports (North and South).

Table 5.2 *Relative proportion of arms imports and exports in North and South, 1963-82*

| Year | North | | South | |
	Imports %	Exports %	Imports %	Exports %
1963	50	97	50	3
1964	53	97	47	3
1965	45	94	55	6
1966	33	96	67	4
1967	34	96	66	4
1968	32	96	68	4
1969	34	97	66	3
1970	28	96	72	4
1971	27	96	73	4
1972	29	91	71	9
1973	26	98	74	2
1974	28	97	72	3
1975	27	95	73	5
1976	26	95	74	5
1977	22	96	78	4
1978	20	95	80	5
1979	19	95	81	5
1980	21	94	79	6
1981	20	91	80	9
1982	18	87	82	13

Source: USACDA "World Military Expenditures and Arms Transfers"; 1963-73 data from publication no. 74, p. 72; 1972-82 data from publication no. 117 (April 1984), p. 53.

Table 5.3 *Absolute increases[a] in arms and exports in North and South, 1963-73 and 1972-82*

| | 1963-73 | | 1972-82 | |
	Imports %	Exports %	Imports %	Exports %
World	97	97	71	69
North	−36	98	08	60
South	229	81	95	155

[a] Derived by $\frac{1973-1963}{1963}$ and $\frac{1982-1972}{1972}$

Source: Same as for Table 5.2.

Table 5.4 Percent of total exports originating in major exporting countries[a]

Country	1963	'64	'65	'66	'67	'68	'69	'70	'71	'72	'73	'74	'75	'76	'77	'78	'79	'80	'81	'82
U.K.	7	5	3	3	2	3	3	1	3	4	5	5	4	4	4	6	5	7	8	6
U.S.	37	35	40	42	46	52	61	54	55	38	37	39	38	35	34	28	24	23	24	26
France	3	5	3	5	2	4	4	3	3	7	6	6	5	7	6	8	6	10	12	9
USSR	38	35	33	33	36	27	18	26	24	28	40	35	31	32	33	33	43	36	29	30
Total	85	80	79	83	86	86	86	84	85	77	88	85	78	78	77	75	78	76	73	71
North[b]	97	97	94	96	96	96	97	96	96	91	98	97	95	95	96	95	95	94	91	87

Country Exports
  Total World Exports
[a] Total North (developed) exports.
Source: Same as for Table 5.2.

5.4   Commodity exports and arms imports

As most arms are purchased by the South, and approximately 80% of the South's exports are primary commodities, it is reasonable to expect a connection between arms imports and commodity prices and exports: In substantial measure North–South trade can be characterized as a trade of raw materials and minerals for capital goods and arms.

There is in fact a strong statistical relationship between the revenues that a number of Southern countries receive from commodity exports and their expenditures on armaments imports. For example, a significant fraction of the increase in the U.S. oil import bill between 1972 and 1974 subsequently returned to the United States as arms exports to the Middle East.

Table 5.5 gives a more precise analysis of this relationship. It reports relationships between commodity export revenues and arms imports for Brazil, Chile, Cuba, Ghana, India, Indonesia, Ivory Coast, Pakistan, Saudi Arabia, Thailand, and Turkey. In this group, Saudi Arabia and Indonesia export oil, Brazil and Ivory Coast export coffee, India tea, Cuba sugar, Ghana cocoa, Pakistan and Thailand rice, Chile copper, and Turkey exports cotton. The group therefore includes exporters of fuels, minerals, and of most internationally traded agricultural commodities produced by developing countries.

The figures reported in Table 5.5 are based on a data set running from 1963 to 1982. They show the results of regressions of armaments imports on commodity export revenues over this period for the above countries. Both in terms of time period and countries covered, the sample was dictated by data availability.

The results show that in every case studied, allowing for lags, the coefficient of the value of arms imports on commodity export revenues is positive and, in a statistical sense, very significantly greater than zero. Furthermore, they show that it is possible to explain a significant fraction of the variation in expenditures on arms imports by changes in commodity export revenues: This fraction varies from a minimum of 58–9% in the case of Turkey to a maximum of 95–8% in the case of Saudi Arabia, with an average over the ten countries of 81–6%.

5.5   Conclusions

Trade in armaments is now as much a part of North–South trade as trade in oil or other commodities; indeed, there is a close relationship between the two. Most arms exports originate in the North: the United States, the

Table 5.5. *Relationships between commodity export revenues and arms imports*[a]

Country	Constant (t-stat)	a_1 (t-stat)	a_2 (t-stat)	a_3 (t-stat)	R^2
Brazil	−2.60 (−1.75)	0.88 (2.58)			0.634
Chile	−53.8 (−3.84)	0.107 (8.24)			0.798 0.798
Cuba	−0.207 (−0.011)	0.056 (5.07)			0.622
Ghana	−10.3 (−2.61)	0.058 (6.14)			0.670
India	−149.1 (−2.00)	1.50 (6.10)			0.681
Indonesia	−27.4 (−1.99)	−0.02 (−0.48)	0.06 (1.1)	0.15 (4.3)	0.918
Ivory Coast	−14.2 (−1.65)	0.058 (5.61)			0.616
Pakistan	27.56 (1.89)	0.084 (1.12)	−0.02 (−0.13)	0.42 (3.79)	0.884
Saudi Arabia	−44.15 (−0.76)	0.003 (1.21)	0.021 (7.67)		0.958
Thailand	−21.8 (−1.40)	0.047 (1.09)	0.092 (2.08)		0.820
Turkey	148.0 (3.60)	0.498 (3.37)			0.589

[a] Equation reported:
Value of arms imports(t) = constant
$+ a_1 \cdot$ commodity export revenues(t)
$+ a_2 \cdot$ commodity export revenues($t - 1$)
$+ a_3 \cdot$ commodity export revenues($t - 2$).

United Kingdom, France, and the Soviet Union account for about 90% of the world's exports. Most internationally traded arms are purchased by the South. The concentration in the armaments market exceeds that in the oil market. Armaments trade recycles to the North some of its expenditures on commodity imports from the South.

There exists a stable and significant propensity to spend export revenues on arms imports in Southern countries; this works against their realization of any potential gains from increased exports.

CHAPTER 6

Aid, trade, and debt

6.1   Aid: the background

Transfers from the North to the South have been widely discussed as a means of narrowing the wealth gap between the two regions. As early as 1961, the industrial market economies agreed to a target donation of 1% of their GNP to poor nations, with 0.7% in the form of Official Development Assistance (ODA), that is, concessional transfers from or guaranteed by governments.[1] The matter received widespread attention; it became a permanent feature of North–South dialogues, and many economic models of North–South relations saw it as the single most important policy tool for narrowing the wealth gap.[2]

However, in recent years the issue of North–South transfers has lost some of its appeal. It is becoming increasingly clear that North–South aid flows are following a downward trend. They never reached even 30% of the stated goals, and in recent years have decreased significantly in absolute as well as in relative terms, except for the OPEC countries' contributions.[3] Table 6.1 gives ODA as a percentage of GNP for major aid donors and illustrates these facts.

Since their recent economic recession, industrial countries have shown little wish to consider the matter of transfers, and the issue has effectively been dropped from the North–South agenda. In addition to the decline in ODA, contributions to other development assistance programs have also

[1] See, for example, Jan Tinbergen (coord.), *RIO* (Reshaping the International Order), New York, E.P. Dutton, 1976, pp. 35–6.

[2] See, for instance, the discussion in A. Carter, W. Leontief, and P. Petri, *The Future of the World Economy,* United Nations, 1976. Their study estimated the possible magnitudes involved in larger foreign aid flows to narrow the North–South wealth gap: "The gross aid ratio would increase from 0.85 percent in 1970 to 1 percent in 1980 and 2 percent in 2,000 in North America" pp. 45–6. See also the discussion in the Bariloche model, which introduced the concept of basic needs and, by contrast, questioned the role of such transfers in reaching these goals. For instance, see G. Chichilnisky, "Development Patterns and the International Order," *Journal of International Affairs* (1979), or A. Herrera, G. Chichilnisky, et al., *Catastrophe or New Society,* IDRC, Ottawa, Canada, 1976 and *Grenzen des Elends,* S. Fischer Verlag GmbH, Frankfurt am Main, 1977, all of which discuss in detail the issue of transfers and basic needs in the context of the Bariloche model.

[3] See *RIO* (op. cit.). Official development assistance from 17 developed market economies has actually declined from 0.52% in 1960 to 0.3% in 1975, see *RIO* fn. 14, Annex 2. See also Brandt Commission, *North–South, A Program for Survival,* MIT Press, Cambridge, Mass., 1980, pp. 224–5.

Table 6.1. *Aid donors: comparison in 1981*

	ODA ($ million)	Share in world ODA (%)	ODA as % of GNP	Per capita income ($)
Arab Gulf states:	7,317	20.4	3.85	16,120
Saudi Arabia	5,658	15.8	4.66	13,040
UAE	799	2.2	2.88	36,040
Kuwait	685	1.9	1.98	23,650
Qatar	175	0.5	2.64	26,520
Iraq	143	0.4	0.37	2,930
Libya	105	0.3	0.37	9,230
Algeria	65	0.2	0.16	2,120
Total Arab donors	7,630	21.3	2.54	6,230
Nigeria	149	0.4	0.17	1,000
Venezuela	67	0.2	0.10	4,790
Iran	−150	−0.4	—	(2,100)
Total OPEC	7,696	21.5	1.40	2,870
United States	5,783	16.2	0.20	12,730
EEC	12,743	35.7	0.53	9,240

Source: Aid from OPEC Countries, OECD 1983, p. 15.

followed a decreasing trend. It now seems unrealistic to place great hopes on aid as a means of narrowing the North–South wealth gap.[4]

Even if aid were to reach its agreed target, it is in fact not clear that the welfare effects on the recipients would be positive. It is quite possible for the receipt of aid to make its recipient worse off. This is the so-called transfer paradox, a classical topic in international economics.

6.2   Transfers and terms of trade

Transfers do not occur in a vacuum, but rather in a market environment. An analysis of the impact of a transfer of wealth is therefore incomplete without an understanding of the reactions of market prices to this transfer. Such prices include the "terms of trade" between the North and the South: They therefore influence such policy concerns as exports, investment, and growth.

A transfer aiming to reduce international disparities in income levels between the North and the South must be very large in magnitude because

[4] OPEC contributions in some cases reached 10% of GNP or more. Details are in *North–South, A Program for Survival,* a report to the Brandt Commission (op. cit.): "A new and important source of aid in the 1970's has been the OPEC members, which supplied about

the wealth differentials are enormous.[5] We can therefore expect such transfers to have a nontrivial impact on a number of economic variables that depend on income levels, and in particular on trade flows and demand patterns in the countries concerned. Such transfers necessarily lead to changes in market prices.

As in the case of export policies discussed in Chapter 4, changes in income have significant effects on patterns of demand. Since transfers change the endowments of the giver and of the receiver, they change their income levels. Income shifts from one group with certain preferences to another group with different preferences. Through these changes in income and demand, transfers affect market prices.

In some cases, the changes in market prices that follow a transfer are more helpful to the donor than to the receiver. Despite its counterintuitive nature, this is in fact a classical proposition in trade theory, going back to the work of Wassily Leontief in 1936.[6] The general problem of the welfare effects of a transfer is one of the oldest in trade theory, starting with the work of John Stuart Mill. How is it that transfers can increase the welfare of the donor and decrease that of the receiver?

Consider a country that imports certain products from another; to fix ideas call these "industrial goods." After receiving the transfer, with its "new wealth," the receiver increases its demand for industrial goods, leading to a rise in their prices. This price effect is the key to the problem. A transfer has a negative effect on the receiver when its effect is to lower the terms of trade of the receiver, that is, to increase the relative prices of the good imported by the receiver. If the price of the imports increases sufficiently, the receiver may find that, despite the expansion of its budget, it is less able to import and to consume than before.[7]

For several years this transfer problem was considered something of a curiosity because it was established that, in a two-country world, it could

20 percent of all Official Development Assistance in 1978. This represents an average of 1.59 percent of their GNP, but individual countries such as Saudi Arabia, Kuwait, U.A.E. and Qatar, have provided between 6 and 15 percent of their GNP in past years and between 4 and 5 percent in 1978" (p. 226).

5 A case where the magnitude of the transfers is not a negligible part of total income is that of the remittances of earnings of citizens employed overseas in certain developing countries. For example, in the cases of Egypt and Pakistan, these remittances were equal in value to 90% of the value of merchandise exports in 1978; see UNCTAD/TDR/2 (Vol. II), para. 169.

6 For a discussion of this literature and of empirical evidence for such effects, see, for example, G. Chichilnisky, "Basic Goods, Commodity Transfers and the International Economic Order," *Journal of Development Economics* 7(4) (1980), and 505–19 and "The Transfer Problem with Three Agents Once Again: Characterization, Uniqueness and Stability," *Journal of Development Economics* 13(1–2) (1983), 237–48.

7 This was shown by W. Leontief in 1936 and in G. Chichilnisky, "Basic Goods, Commodity Transfers and the International Economic Order," op. cit.; see also chapter 12.

only occur in unstable markets.[8] The phenomenon was therefore thought to be at worst rare and temporary. However, it has recently been established that this problem arises very generally in a world economy with three or more trading regions, and that it also occurs in stable markets.[9] The problem may in fact be quite persistent and general.

The main result here is that in a three-region world where a donor makes a transfer to a recipient, the recipient may be worse off whenever the third region, which does not participate in the transfer, imports the products in which the donor specializes. Consider for example a world economy with three regions: an industrial region, a newly industrialized region, and a less developed region. Typically the industrial region makes a transfer to the less developed region; the donor consumes mostly industrial goods and the receiver basic goods. Under these conditions a transfer may make the receiver worse off when the nonparticipant region, namely the newly industrialized region in our example, imports industrial goods. This occurs in markets that are perfectly competitive and stable.[10]

We described a typical case where the conditions for the negative impacts of transfers may be satisfied: When the industrial countries transfer goods or money to the lower-income LDCs, while the newly industrializing countries, which do not participate in the transfer, are net importers of industrial goods. This is clearly a plausible case. Of course, in other cases the results may reverse: The receiver gains, and the giver loses. One can identify the conditions for one or the other outcome to occur.[11]

In sum: A transfer has a negative effect on the recipient when market forces drive up the prices of goods imported by the recipient and drive down the prices of the goods that the recipient exports.[12] The recipient is worse off because its terms of trade are lower: It gets less for what it sells,

---

[8] See R. A. Mundell, "The Pure Theory of International Trade," *American Economic Review* 50(1) (1960), 67–110.

[9] G. Chichilnisky, "Basic Goods, Commodity Transfers and the International Economic Order" (op. cit.) showed for the first time in the literature that the transfer may worsen the welfare of the receiver and improve that of the giver in a stable market.

[10] This precise model is that of a pure exchange economy with three regions, two goods, and limited substitution in the preferences, which emphasizes income effects; see G. Chichilnisky, "Basic Goods, Commodity Transfers and the International Economic Order" (op. cit.). More recent results that strengthen this proposition on transfers are in G. Chichilnisky, "The Transfer Problem with Three Agents Once Again: Characterization, Uniqueness and Stability" (op. cit.). For a discussion of related issues on transfers see also S. Kojima, "Neoclassical Theory of a New International Economic Order: An Asymmetric Two-Country Three-Commodity Approach," Discussion Paper no. 5, UNCTAD, 1982, and Chapter 12 of the present work.

[11] For a discussion, see also J. Geanakoplos and G. Heal, "The Transfer Paradox in a Stable Economy," Cowles Foundation for Economic Research Working Paper, Yale University, 1982 and *Journal of Development Economics* 13(1–2) (1983), 223–36.

[12] A transfer may have a negative impact quite independently of the *denomination* of the transfer, which can be in industrial goods, in consumption goods, or in money.

and it must pay more for what it buys. The donor, on the other hand, owns less after the transfer, but the market value of what it owns is higher because of the change in prices.

This discussion does not condemn aid as a useless or perverse policy tool. However, it serves as a warning: It is unrealistic to expect that transfers will always decrease wealth differentials when the welfare of the countries concerned depends on their positions in the international market and on their international terms of trade. These may be affected positively or negatively by the transfer.

6.3   When will aid help?

Certain economic policies could offset the negative impacts of a transfer. Negative results may be avoided by appropriate supply responses. For example, the welfare losses that derive from higher import prices may be checked if domestic producers increase their production of importable goods as a response to the higher prices of these goods. A drop in imports could then be offset by higher levels of domestic output, employment, and consumption.

Consider the rather general case where the LDC receiving the transfer imports food from the North. The transfer may lead to increased demand, and thus higher prices, of the imported food. However, the negative impact of higher food prices, which lowers the volume of food imported and the domestic consumption of food, may be offset by increases in domestic production of food. This positive output response is consistent with profit-maximizing behavior: Food producers can naturally be expected to increase supplies when faced with higher food prices.

What is at stake here is the relative strength of supply and demand responses. A positive output response may offset the negative effect of higher prices on demand. This suggests once more the importance of measures addressed to improving productivity in the agricultural or subsistence sector of developing countries.

In sum, the correction of underconsumption and of inequalities cannot be based solely on aid flows. Aid does not improve the basic difficulties of the economy and may in some cases lead to more unfavorable conditions. If aid does not raise productivity, the country's terms of trade after the transfer may actually worsen.

Transfer policies share with export-promotion policies a misunderstanding about what constitutes an engine of development: Both rely on engines located outside the region. Sustainable development requires an indigenous engine: an increase in domestic productivity accompanied by stronger domestic markets. A more balanced view of development is required, one that sees the domestic population not just as a input whose costs are to be minimized, but rather as an important component of the market demand itself. This is akin to widely accepted prescriptions for industrial economies: The need to increase productivity and output is emphasized by supply side economists, whereas the need to strengthen domestic markets is a traditional Keynesian prescription. Both demand and supply sides are important. This wisdom should also be applied to the developing countries.

6.4   Lending to LDCs: origins of the problem

While aid and concessional or "soft" loans to the developing countries have decreased in recent years, commercial banks' lending to these countries has risen dramatically. In the past couple of years, the international financial community has become acutely concerned about the substantial foreign debt accumulated by some developing countries, a significant part of which is outstanding loans from private institutions in industrial countries.[13] In part, these loans represented a recycling of OPEC revenues, which were deposited in the commercial banks of industrial nations.[14] Table 6.2 gives details of these flows.

Several factors led to the current debt crisis. The severity of the last recession in the industrial countries decreased these countries' demands for loanable funds. Coupled with the increases in OPEC deposits, this led to an excess of loanable funds. A number of these banks then provided large loans to developing countries. These countries managed to maintain higher investment and growth rates than the industrial countries in the aggregate, adding some impetus to the world economy[15] and providing an

---

[13] See Felix G. Rohatyn, "The State of the Banks," *New York Review of Books:* "According to the Federal Reserve, as of May 1982, U.S. banks have loaned over $300 billion abroad. This includes $200 billion in Latin America, the Third World and Eastern Europe. To put these numbers in perspective, it is worth noting that the total equity of the thirty largest U.S. bank holding companies as of mid-1982, i.e., the value of their assets over their total liabilities, was about $40 billion. American banks are major participants in Mexico's $80 billion of external debt, as well as Brazil's $60 billion and Argentina's $40 billion; the risk to American banks of an unexpected default by these and other countries would therefore be grave ones" (pp. 5–6). (Reprinted with permission from the *New York Review of Books.* Copyright © NYREV, 1982.)

[14] See J. D. Sachs, "The Current Account and Macroeconomic Adjustment in the 1970s,"*Brookings Papers on Economic Activity* 1 (1981), 201–82, for an analysis of the consequences of OPEC surpluses for patterns of borrowing and lending.

[15] Out of eighty-eight developing countries for which data are available, forty-six achieved an average GNP growth of 4.5% or higher between 1970 and 1979 compared with an average 3.2% for the industrial economies. About a third exceeded 6% per annum (see World Bank, *World Development Report 1981,* Oxford University Press, New York). Investment as a proportion of GNP in LDCs increased from 15.7 for 1960 to 23.6 in 1978. By contrast, the U.S. figures are about 16%-17% from 1965 to 1979. Sources are Interna-

apparently profitable outlet for loans. The enterprising spirit of capitalism, in the form of commercial bank loans, therefore provided a measure of liquidity much needed at a time when the governments of industrial countries would not provide an equivalent. However, bank loans are rather short-term, typically two to five years, and often underwritten with floating interest rates.

In the four years preceding 1980, interest rates in the United States and the United Kingdom increased threefold as a consequence of their restrictive monetary policies.[16] Only in recent years have they declined somewhat, and they are still more than twice their 1976 levels. Increases in interest rates were initiated in part as a domestic policy response to oil price increases. A restrictive monetary policy was the official U.S. and U.K. response to the fear of inflation in an era of high oil prices. Their interest rates soared, and those of other countries followed in an attempt to control outflows of capital.

Since the United States and the United Kingdom are the home bases of many of the commercial banks, the burden of debt increased very significantly for many LDCs, which borrowed at floating rates. For example, Mexico, Argentina, and Brazil contracted a large part of their loans on the basis of floating interest rates. To illustrate the orders of magnitude involved, with $300 billion debt (which is the approximate debt of Latin American countries) a one-point increase in interest rates represents $3 billion in extra repayments or additions to the debt. A twelve-point rise from 6% to 18% therefore represents a threefold increase in the costs of debt servicing, from $18 billion p.a. to $54 billion p.a., giving demands on the balance of payments of $36 billion p.a. The change in domestic monetary policies in major industrial countries therefore seriously undermined the ability of borrowing nations to service existing debts. This problem continues.

In addition to having floating rates, developing countries' loans are due for repayment after periods that by historical standards are very short for major international loans. This has also increased the financial pressures on the borrowers: Large capital sums became due for repayment or renegotiation early in the lives of the loans, and at particularly difficult times for the borrowers. Longer terms would have allowed greater flexibility in the choice of circumstances for renegotiation. These loans are short because they were made by commercial banks, rather than being raised by

tional Monetary Fund, *International Financial Statistics,* and OECD, *National Accounts for OECD Countries, 1950-78,* Paris, 1980. See also J. Sachs, *Brookings Papers in Economic Activity* (op. cit.), Tables 9 and 10, who discusses also the recycling of OPEC surpluses as loans to developing countries that had high rates of investment and growth.

[16] In fact, because of the decline in inflation rates in the United States, real interest rates rose even more sharply.

Table 6.2. *Estimated development of OPEC countries, investable surplus, 1974–81 ($ billions)*

	1974	1974	1976	1977	1978	1979	1980	1981	1982
Identified investable surplus[a]	53.2	35.2	35.7	33.5	13.4	61.3	87.0	43.2	3.1
Short-term investments	36.6	9.5	10.2	10.2	3.2	43.2	42.5	4.9	−16.2
of which in:									
U.S.[b]	9.4	1.1	0.7	−0.5	−0.2	8.3	0.2	−3.5	4.8
U.K.[b]	18.2	3.4	3.0	3.2	−1.6	16.2	16.1	7.9	−8.2
of which in:									
(Eurocurrency deposits)	(13.8)	(4.1)	(5.6)	(3.1)	(−2.0)	(14.8)	(14.8)	(8.1)	(−9.4)
Other indust. countries[c]	9.0	5.0	6.5	7.5	5.0	18.7	26.2	0.5	−12.8
Long-term investments	17.3	29.0	25.5	23.3	10.2	18.1	44.5	38.3	19.3
of which in:									
U.S.	2.3	8.5	7.2	7.4	0.2	−1.5	14.3	15.3	7.6
U.K.	2.8	0.9	1.4	0.6	−0.2	1.0	2.0	0.1	−0.8
Other indust. countries[c]	3.1	5.8	4.3	5.8	2.6	8.7	16.7	13.6	6.6

[a] The difference between current-account position and identified foreign investment reflects, apart from recording errors, borrowing (net of repayments) by OPEC countries, direct investment inflows, trade credits, and other unidentified capital flows.
[b] Including bank deposits and money-market placements.
[c] Bank deposits only.
Source: Bank of England Quarterly Bulletin (June 1982).

government bond issues, as was often the case with earlier rounds of international borrowing.[17]

Another issue that has increased the financial pressures on the borrower nations was the rise in the value of the U.S. dollar in 1982, 1983, and 1984, – a rise that was, of course, connected to the extremely high levels of U.S. real interest rates. The debts of the developing countries are largely denominated in U.S. dollars, and the rise in the dollar relative to other currencies has raised the nondollar export earnings needed to service and repay their debts. All of this – high interest rates and a high U.S. dollar – occurred at a time when export opportunities for the borrowers were particularly limited, as pointed out in Chapters 3 and 4. Exports of basic manufactures are encountering increasing protectionism, and primary commodity prices are at an all-time low in real terms.

The pressure on debtor countries to increase exports in order to service their debts contributes to the current excess supplies in commodity markets and to the low commodity prices. This pressure also contributes to the market penetration of developing countries in fields such as textiles, steel, and footware and increases protectionist resistance in the industrial countries. It contributes also to the current drop in dollar-denominated oil prices, which affects rather negatively large debtor countries such as Mexico and, by implication, the international banking community.

The past century has seen several international financial crises associated with problems in the repayment of international loans, but the present crisis is probably the most severe of these and the most far-reaching in its ramifications.[18]

6.5   Debt and interdependence

The picture so far is rather negative, but it may be recognized that the impact of U.S. and U.K. monetary policies was profound and may have set in motion short- and long-term changes in the international financial system. We have already been able to observe some of these changes. The recent 47% increase in IMF quotas is a rather striking example. The Inter-American Development Bank has also recently voted to increase its loans by 30%. Lately more flexible policies have been adopted by the U.S. government and banking system toward Latin American borrowers. All this indicates an understanding of the new degree of interdependence of

---

[17] For an elaboration of this point, see W. Arthur Lewis, *The Evolution of the International Economic Order,* Princeton, 1978, chaps. 7–9.
[18] W. A. Lewis (op. cit.) has a discussion of the present problems in the context of their predecessors.

the world's financial system: Both the borrowers and the lenders wish to avoid disruptive outcomes.

Effects that are more indirect, but not less striking, are also being felt at present. The very enterprising nature of the industrial countries' banking systems provided a check to monetarist experiments of the U.S. and U.K. governments. The exposure of the banks in these countries led them to press for a realistic ceiling on interest rates and for a more accommodating monetary policy.

The private banking system, an important bastion of capitalism, became rather vulnerable to precisely those developing countries that had borrowed from it. It has been noted that "Third World countries recently attained unprecedented leverage because of their ability to harm the western banking system."[19] This provides an object lesson in international interdependence: Banks' recycling of OPEC funds led them to press for easier credit policies within the United States because their own survival depended on the ability of their international borrowers to continue paying.

Both the symbolic and the real aspects of this crisis have been profoundly educational. The high interest rates that were partly a response to OPEC pricing policies eventually gave more leverage to the third world through the debt issue. Argentina and Brazil recently proposed rescheduling of part of their debts on favorable and somewhat novel terms, and their proposals were reluctantly accepted because of their inevitability. Since then, negotiations between Mexico and the banking community have led to a similar outcome.

Under the circumstances, any attempt to alleviate the debt crisis necessarily contributes as much to bracing the viability of the international banking system as to any other aim; it was in part this consideration that recently moved the United States to support a 47% increase in the IMF quotas – an increase that was historically unprecedented and that under different circumstances might not have been achieved by many years of North–South negotiations.

There have been a number of proposals for increasing international liquidity, some reflecting a similar concern for the viability of the existing financial system, and others expressing concerns for the borrowing countries.[20] Obviously the external debt has very serious impacts on countries such as Mexico, Brazil, and Argentina: There are high costs to the painful

[19] *Financial Times*, Editorial, 12 February 1983, p. 16.

[20] See, for example, M. M. Sakbani, "A Critique of the Prevailing Monetary System: Principal Themes of a Reformed System," *Third World Quarterly* 3(3) (July 1981), 460–72, and D. Avramovic, "The Developing Countries After Cancun," *Journal of World Trade Law* 16(1) (Jan/Feb 1982), 3–26.

austerity programs imposed by the IMF as conditions for helping the major Latin American debtor countries. However, it is equally obvious that the survival of states is less dependent on the repayment of their debt than is the survival of the lending banks. The crisis has clearly precipitated an understanding of the need to renegotiate some of the debt.

The debt crisis also contains an important lesson for debtor countries that followed export-led strategies based either on more traditional commodities, such as Brazil and Argentina, or on oil, such as Mexico, Ecuador, and Venezuela. As the international sectors of their economies expanded rapidly, and often inefficiently, their imports from industrial countries soared and exceeded the revenues from increased exports. Furthermore, concentration on their export sectors led them to neglect their subsistence sectors, which contracted, and to a consequent dependence on food imports, as in the case of Venezuela.[21] The lesson is that development strategies based mostly on resource exports have very high risks because their success is tied to the international terms of trade for primary commodities, which are notoriously volatile and unreliable. For example, the recent drop in the price of oil had severe consequences for the Mexican economy, which had been oriented to depend to a great extent on the production and export of oil, following a conventional and now dated view of development strategies.

The debt problem underscores the overall concern with the management of the world's monetary system.[22] This concern arises in part from the effects of the strict monetarist regimes imposed by leading industrial economies in an attempt to combat their domestic inflation. In this context, the issue of transfers to developing countries has been replaced by a concern to develop better international financial tools. These are intended to alleviate deficits and the crippling interest payments on debts, as well as to forestall the instability of financial institutions in the industrial countries with a very significant exposure.

There is a general unease about the adequacy of existing international institutions, some of which are acknowledged to be dated, going back as far as the immediate postwar years.[23] While the international community

---

21 In the early 1980s Venezuela imported 60% of the food it consumed.
22 "The predicament has fueled thinking about new mechanisms of international finance," including "A new superagency of trade, long term interest bonds for some of the sovereign debts that have been piled up in bank portfolios," and "the creation of a new international agency, backed by central banks instead of institutions like the International Monetary Fund." The agency could "swap noninterest-bearing bonds backed by central banks for troublesome loans. The banks getting the bonds could hold on to them and treat them as assets equal in face value to the loans but assets that do not require the setting aside of funds to cover the possible failure of debtors to repay." "The World Banking Crisis," Section F, *New York Times*, 27 March, 1983. (Copyright © 1983 by The New York Times Company. Reprinted by permission.)
23 See M. M. Sakbani, "A Critique of the Prevailing Monetary System" (op. cit.).

discusses the possibility of updating its monetary and financial institutions, the recent changes in the world economy strain the capacities of existing ones to cope with the demands of the day. The emergence of newer and more adequate institutional arrangements is anticipated[24]; however, an active role for the developing countries in the restructuring of the international financial system seems necessary to forestall future crises.

6.6   Debt and the lenders

To obtain a complete perspective on the international debt issue, we have to look not just at the effects of the debt on the borrowers and on the banks, but also at its effects on the overall international macroeconomic situation. In particular we should look at the effects that these loans had on *lending* countries.

For example, in the case of lending by U.S. banks to Mexico, there were two effects on the U.S. economy, other than the direct capital movements from the U.S. to Mexico and the subsequent repayments of capital and interest. One effect was the provision of cheaper oil to the U.S. economy. This happened because a significant fraction of the borrowed funds was used to finance the development of the Mexican oil sector: Although it is difficult to trace in detail the disposition of the borrowed funds, statistical analysis suggests that for every dollar of foreign debt accumulated, about eighty cents were invested in the national oil company, Petroleos Mexicanos (PEMEX). Figure 6.1 shows the data on which this analysis is based. As a result of this investment, Mexican oil exports rose rapidly (Figure 6.2), and this rapid growth in the output of a non-OPEC supplier was one of the important factors that contributed to the softening of prices in the world oil market in the early 1980s. In fact, as Figure 4.4(b) shows, from 1980 to 1983 Mexico's oil exports were rising as its oil prices fell. Of course, the softening of oil prices benefited the United States, the lending economy. The United States' import bill decreased, its terms of trade improved, and there was a sharp rise in the profitability of sectors sensitive to energy prices, such as transportation and automobiles. One of the consequences of the accumulation of debt in Mexico was therefore the provision of cheaper oil to the United States and to other industrial countries.

Indeed, loans made by industrial countries to developing countries are often made to develop overseas sources of exportable resources. This

[24] Dissatisfaction with "the disorderly world monetary system" is expressed in L. Silk, "Seeking a New Bretton Woods," *New York Times,* 25 March 1983, p. D2. The Group of Ten is conducting discussions about the need for replacement for the Bretton Woods agreement.

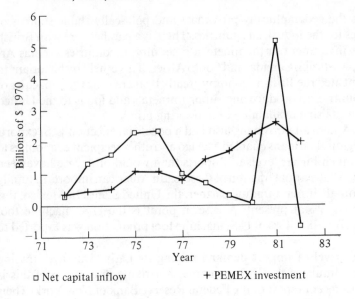

Figure 6.1. Net capital inflow and PEMEX investment.

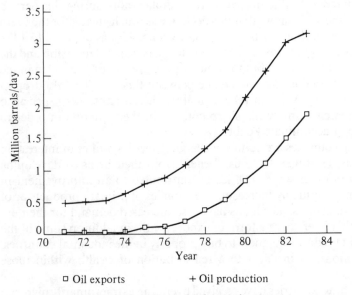

Figure 6.2. Mexican oil production and exports.

expands the geographically proximate and politically stable sources of resources for the industrial countries. There is a parallel here with British overseas investment in the nineteenth century in countries such as Argentina, Australia, Canada, and South Africa. This is held by historians to have benefited the British economy greatly by increasing the capacities of these countries to produce and supply minerals and foods to the United Kingdom, raising availability and lowering prices.

Latin American borrowing also had a beneficial effect on U.S. exports to the region. The loans enabled Mexico and other recipient economies to sustain much higher levels of imports than would otherwise have been possible. A substantial fraction of these Latin American imports naturally came from their main trading partner, the United States. In Mexico, this fraction is 75% at present. A case in point is the U.S. machine tool industry. By 1983, 40% of U.S. machine tool production was exported to Mexico.

A high level of import demand among its Latin American trading partners stimulates the U.S. economy. A striking illustration of this is given by a recent report of the Federal Reserve Bank of New York. Their calculations indicate that in 1983 the cutback in imports due to the debt crisis led to a drop in U.S. exports to the region sharp enough to cause a rise in unemployment of at least 250,000 within the United States.

Table 6.3 throws further light on this same issue, showing the behavior of various categories of U.S. exports over the period 1981–3. All categories registered a decline in their current dollar value during this period. However, the table shows that this decline was much greater for the Latin America region than for the world as a whole: 42% as opposed to 14%. U.S. exports might have been expected to fall because of recession and the high value of the dollar, but these factors are presumably reflected in the 14% overall decline. The difference between this and the 42% drop in exports to Latin America reflects mainly the circumstances special to Latin America, namely the sharp cutback in their imports in order to service their accumulated debt.

Lending countries are certainly charging very high rates of interest on their loans. However, they also benefit from their loans to developing countries in other ways. The loans contributed to an improvement in their terms of trade by increasing the supplies of primary products or of basic manufactures. The loans have also increased demand for their exports, acting in effect as a form of export credit. In addition some of the loans were used by foreigners to buy property in the industrial countries, and so amounted in effect to a redistribution of wealth within those countries.

The lending countries have received overall an extraordinarily high rate of return: The debtor countries now coping with IMF-imposed austerity

Table 6.3. *U.S. exports to Latin America and to the world*

	Exports to world decline			Exports to Latin America decline			Latin American share of decline in U.S. world exports
	1981	1983	1981–3	1981	1983	1981–3	1981–3
	($ billions)		(%)	($ billions)		(%)	
Total	233.7	200.5	−14	39.0	22.6	−42	49
Selected areas:							
Manufactured goods	154.3	132.5	−14	29.7	15.2	−49	67
Machinery & transport. equip.	95.7	82.6	−14	17.8	8.2	−54	73
Automobiles	7.9	4.6	−42	3.6	1.5	−54	65
Civilian aircraft	13.5	10.7	−21	1.8	0.8	−57	37
Construction equip.	6.3	2.4	−62	1.5	0.3	−79	31
Agricultural machinery	3.5	1.6	−54	0.7	0.1	−86	29

Source: U.S. Department of Commerce; Bureau of Census.

programs must have a clear impression of the dangers of relying on short-term liquidity and the need to change the international financial system.

The asymmetric outcome of these loans can be predicted on theoretical grounds,[25] although theoretical analysis suggests that the outcome could also be a more equitable division of the benefits from the loan under suitable conditions. The issue is closely related to the transfer problem already discussed. In both cases the question is whether a transfer of resources from one country to another will necessarily benefit the recipient. In one case the transfer is a loan and has to be repaid over several years; in the other it is a gift. However, this does not affect the immediate impact of the transfer. In both cases market effects are induced by the transfer.

[25] See G. Chichilnisksy, G. M. Heal, and D. L. McLeod, "Resources, Trade and Debt: The Case of Mexico," Working Paper No. 1984-4, Division of Global Analysis and Projections, The World Bank.

CHAPTER 7

Resources and North–South trade

7.1 An overview

Extractive resources, and indeed primary commodities in general, have a notorious history of price volatility. In the 1950s and 1960s prices were generally falling in real terms as shown in Figure 7.1(a). The figure also shows that in the 1970s this pattern changed; at the same time there was a shift of market power from consumers to producers. The increase in prices was a response to unprecedentedly high levels of industrial activity by user countries, and to demand conditions generated by decades of low prices. The oil market was, of course, the prime example and set a trail that other commodity producers sought to follow [Figure 7.1(b)]. Here a seller's market enabled OPEC to overcome two decades of market dominance by the buying cartel of major oil companies and to begin for the first time exercising significant market power on behalf of producers. Although in some circles the role of monopoly on the buying side in holding prices down has been noted for years,[1] this point has only lately become very generally accepted. Widely read publications in the United States and the United Kingdom have commented recently that "In one sense the dramatic increase in oil prices in the mid 1970's represented a belated recognition by the producers that the market had been rigged in the Western interest,"[2] and that OPEC was formed initially as "a cartel to confront a cartel."[3]

It has not only been in resource markets that industrial countries have been in a position to exercise market power. On the selling side they have been able to dominate the markets for goods as diverse as food, armaments, and various types of capital goods.[4] This recognition has also dawned on other producers, creating a concern to ensure in the future pricing policies that distribute the gains from resource trade more equitably among buyers and sellers.

[1] This was noted by P. S. Dasgupta and G. M. Heal in *Economic Theory and Exhaustible Resources,* Cambridge University Press, 1979.
[2] *Financial Times,* Editorial, 12 February 1983.
[3] *Newsweek,* 7 March 1983, pp. 62–3.
[4] For details, see G. Chichilnisky, M. de Mello, and A. Roberts, *Two Studies on International Markets,* UNITAR, 1983.

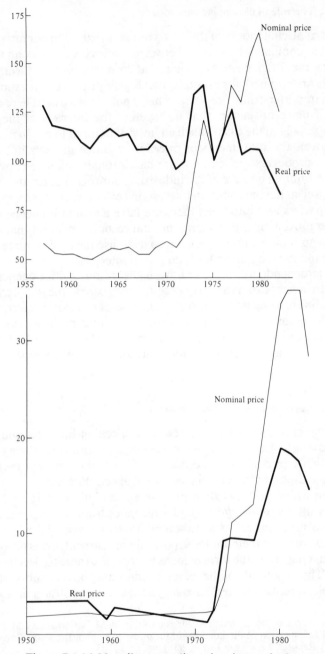

(a)

(b)

Figure 7.1 (a) Nonoil commodity prices in nominal terms and in real terms; (b) crude oil prices in nominal terms (1970 = 100) and deflated by the U.S. GDP deflator. Same as Figures 4.1 and 4.2. *Source:* see Figure 4.1.

The sharp pricing shocks of the 1970s brought sharply to our attention the possible conflicts of interests between resource exporters and importers. It is now often taken as obvious that the interests of producers and consumers are opposed; for example, that higher prices benefit exporters and harm importers, and vice versa. This is not always true: There are a number of powerful factors that tie together the interests of the two parties, especially in the case of such an important input to production as oil. Moreover, the movements of prices in resource markets not only depend on producers' policies but are also strongly influenced by the domestic economic policies of the industrial countries that are the main users.[5] As well as having common interests in certain types of price movements, exporters and importers therefore have a shared influence over these price movements. It is then a natural recommendation that they should design their economic policies so as to use their joint influences over these markets to pursue these common interests.

In an interdependent world economy, higher resource prices, generally supposed to benefit exporters, may in some cases benefit the importers as well. In addition, lower prices, usually seen as beneficial to importers, may also benefit exporters. There are circumstances under which both importers and exporters gain from higher prices, and others under which both gain from lower prices. A mutually desirable price range may emerge.

7.2   Resource prices and the importer

Consider the effects of alternative resource prices on importer and exporter. Looking first at the importer, it is possible to distinguish three ways in which higher prices affect its economy. Two of these benefit the importer, while the third, a more conventional effect, does not.

The most widely acknowledged positive effect of higher prices on the importer is the *recycling effect*. Higher revenues from resource exports return to the importing countries in several ways: as increased demand for their own exports, for their domestic portfolio investment, or, as noted in the previous chapter, in the form of loans to non-oil-exporting developing countries. The magnitude of the recycling effect may be very substantial. For example, recent estimates[6] have suggested that up to 50% of the extra

---

[5] Empirical evidence on this is contained, for example, in M. M. Barrow and G. M. Heal, "Empirical Investigation of the Long-Run Movement of Natural Resources Prices: A Preliminary Report," *Economics Letters* 7(1) (1985), 95–103.

[6] See, for example, Jan F. R. Fabritius and Christian Ettrup Petersen, "OPEC Respending and the Economic Impact of an Increase in the Price of Oil," in *The Impact of Rising Oil Prices on the World Economy,* Lars Matthiessen (ed.), Macmillan Press, New York, 1982.

OPEC revenues after the 1973 oil price increase were recycled to the OECD countries and that the total effects of such spending would have been sufficient, in the absence of other deflationary effects, to prevent a decrease in GNP in those countries. Other estimates suggest that the recycling of OPEC surpluses as loans to non-oil-exporting LDCs has had a very positive effect on their rates of growth and on their rate of investment as a proportion of GNP as well. For instance, in the period 1973–9, investment as a proportion of GNP in LDCs grew from 15.7% to 23.6% and LDCs' investment as a proportion of total world investment rose from 4.9% to 8%.[7]

Another source of common interest is the longer-run *conservation effect*. There is an old saying that "the monopolist is the conservationist's best friend," meaning simply that the higher prices supposed to result from monopoly reduce consumption and aid conservation.[8] There have been widespread concerns about the long-run implications of inefficient patterns of extractive resource use and about the way in which this may tighten global constraints on long-run growth. High prices encourage efficient use and the development of substitutes and so help to prevent long-run shortages. The industrial countries, as the main users of resources, are also main beneficiaries of this conservation. This is another reason why higher prices may be of interest to both importer and exporter.

The most important source of community of interest between the importer and exporter is, however, less obvious. It arises from the impact of prices on the employment of factors in the importing country. It is most readily illustrated by reference to the effects of oil prices; however, identical arguments can be made for any imported primary input.

An increase in the price of imported oil leads to a drop in the demand for oil and to increases in the demands for other inputs, such as domestic capital and labor. Producers, seeking minimum cost, change the factor mix so as to use more labor or capital, whose price has not risen, and less of the imported resource.[9] Alternatively, there is a shift toward products that make less use of oil and more use of other inputs. At constant output levels, this raises the employment of domestic capital and labor. The returns to capital and labor therefore increase, and so does national income. At the same time, consumers also change their demand patterns. They turn away from resource-intensive goods, whose prices have risen, and toward goods made mainly from other less expensive inputs, such as

---

[7] For example, J. D. Sachs, "The Current Account and Macroeconomic Adjustment in the 1970s,"*Brookings Papers on Economic Activity* (1981), 201–82.

[8] C. Doblin, *Options,* "Energy Savings and Conservation," (Autumn 1982), IIASA discussed inter alia the negative impact of today's lower oil prices on conservation.

[9] Between 1973 and 1983 the amount of energy used in producing $1,000 of real GNP in the United States fell by 38.9%.

domestic capital and labor. This again tends to increase the employment of, and the rewards to, domestic capital and labor.

In the medium run, therefore, the increase in the price of a resource may increase the employment and remuneration of those domestic factors that can be substituted for it. This is obviously a positive effect as far as the importing economy is concerned. We refer to this as the *factor use effect.*

There is, of course, an immediate *wealth effect,* which is negative: The importing economy must pay more for any given quantity of the resource. Real wealth is reduced by an increase in the price of an import. This drop in real wealth may, however, be checked by other changes in market prices. The resource-importing country's own exports may increase in price in response to the rise in its import prices. This reduces the drop in the terms of trade of the imports. This point is of practical relevance: After the oil price increases of both 1973 and 1979, the prices of OECD industrial exports to OPEC countries increased by amounts quite sufficient to compensate for as much as one-third of the loss of wealth from the higher oil prices.[10] The negative impact of the wealth effect may therefore be significantly reduced by price responses in the importing country. However, in general the wealth effect will reduce domestic demand and thereby reduce the employment of domestic factors. This contractionary consequence of the higher oil price must be offset against other possible beneficial consequences.

Which of these several effects will dominate? As one might expect, there is no general answer to this problem: No effect will uniformly dominate the others; each will predominate at a different set of initial prices. The positive factor use effect will be more important at low prices; the negative wealth effect more so at high prices; and the positive recycling effect will predominate when revenues are high. At intermediate prices their relative magnitudes will switch in a way that depends upon the structural characteristics of the economy. Although there are no general statements about the dominance of wealth and factor employment effects at all price levels, one can nevertheless make the following statement. At low resource prices, the factor employment effect may dominate, with the importing country gaining from an increase in prices. At high prices, instead, the negative wealth effect may dominate: The importing country will gain from a price reduction. At intermediate ranges, the results require precise examination of the economic parameters of the importing country. This leads to a simple conclusion: Both very low and very high resource prices

[10] See G. Heal and G. Chichilnisky, *Oil in the International Economy,* Oxford University Press, London, in press.

are undesirable. There exists therefore an intermediate range that is more favorable to the importers.[11]

Such evidence as is available is quite consistent with our analysis, though insufficient to make a definite judgment. It is only thirteen years since the first large oil price rise, and indeed only eight years or less since the consequences of this became evident. Thirteen or fewer observations provide insufficient evidence for testing a theory. However, to the extent that this theory is based on standard assumptions about market economies, its conclusions seem robust.

The effects of resource price changes on the importer are complex and depend on, among other things, the initial price level. How do these theoretical findings compare with the empirical evidence?

The impact of higher oil prices on the industrial countries is an issue that has been discussed very extensively indeed. The initial discussions placed a large part of the responsibility for the OECD inflation and recession of the mid 1970s on the 1973 oil price increase, and indeed one still finds some support for this view in the press.

More recently, scientific studies of the 1973 price increase have led to a reevaluation. It has been recognized that the problems of inflation and unemployment in the OECD were becoming serious even before 1973,[12] and that the 1973 price increase served to reinforce an existing trend, rather than to introduce a qualitative change. Several studies[13] suggest that the total impact of the 1973 price rise was to raise the price level in the OECD countries by about 6% in total and the level of unemployment by about two percentage points. Recall that, during the mid 1970s, unemployment levels and inflation rates were both in double digits; these effects are thus significant but by no means large.

In addition to these studies of the macroeconomic impact of higher oil prices, there are several interesting studies of the relationship between the demand for energy and the demands for other inputs, in particular capital and labor.[14] These studies proceed by looking at the changes in demands for energy and other inputs resulting from energy price changes. Similar studies have been conducted on different countries and have reached different conclusions: In particular, the relationships between demands

---

[11] These issues are analyzed fully in the references given in footnote 16 below.

[12] See "Inflation – the Present Problem," OECD, Paris, December 1970.

[13] These results are contained in G. E. J. Llewelwyn (Head, Economic Prospects Division, OECD), "Resource Prices and Macroeconomic Policies: Lessons from Two Oil Price Shocks." The paper was presented at the OPEC–UNITAR seminar at Essex University, January 1983. See also W. D. Nordhaus, "Oil Shocks and Economic Activity," *Brookings Papers on Economic Activity* (1981).

[14] These issues, and the relevant literature, are reviewed in G. Chichilnisky and G. M. Heal, "Capital–Energy Substitution: A General Equilibrium Approach," IIASA Collaborative Paper, 1983.

for energy and for other inputs seem to be different in Western Europe and in North America. This is consistent with our theory, in which we argued that the response of factor demands to a rise in oil prices may depend upon the initial level of oil prices and may change as this level changes. The evidence of different relationships between factor demands and energy prices in Europe and North America is quite consistent with this. Energy prices in Europe have traditionally been much higher than those in North America. We can therefore expect different demand responses in Europe and in North America, and this is what is observed.

Furthermore, in the period from 1950 onward, which is the period for which good data are available, there are subperiods, before and after 1973, with very different oil price levels. Therefore, there should be rather different macroeconomic responses to increases in oil prices in each subperiod. This is a hopeful direction of inquiry, but it unfortunately meets with practical difficulties. Most studies of the macroeconomic impact of oil price movements have treated the whole period from 1950 on as one; indeed, the limited number of years since 1973 gives them little choice in this respect. This means that their findings represent an *average* of two different responses. If these responses are in opposite directions, they may each be quite large, and yet their average may be small. The results of studies that average both subperiods could therefore be misleading, underestimating the effects of oil price changes. We do observe small impacts of oil prices in several studies.[15] In any event, whether they find a small overall effect because this is indeed what happened, or because they are averaging two larger but opposite effects, these studies are quite consistent with our analysis, though far from definitive.

7.3   The market position of resource exporters

Like the importer, an exporting country will also gain in some respects not only from an increase in prices when prices are low, but also from a decrease in prices when they are high. This provides the basis for arguing that there is a "cooperative band" of resource prices. Whenever prices are outside this range, both importer and exporter gain by moving into it. If both traders are aware of the full consequences of different pricing strategies, they will both wish to raise prices if they are lower than this band, or reduce them if they are higher. The extent of this price band is, of course, of great practical importance. It is of interest that the theory allows us to

---

[15] Examples are W. D. Nordhaus, "Oil and Economic Performance in Industrial Countries," *Brookings Papers on Economic Activity* 2(1980), 341–99, and G. E. J. Llewelwyn, "Resource Price Shocks and Macroeconomic Policies"(op. cit.).

express this band analytically in terms of the technologies of the regions and to compute it numerically.

This proposition about cooperative price bands has several implications. One is that a free resource may be of less value to an economy than one that is somewhat costly but that, because of this, generates more economic activity. It is as if the challenge of a costly resource spurs the economy to higher levels of activity, provided the cost is not so high as to become crippling. The question of what price is too high or too low in this sense can be answered with precision in technical terms. A second implication is that prices that are too high can harm the *exporter* because of the market responses to these prices, such as significant changes in the economy of the resource-using country; this too can be expressed with precision in technical terms.[16]

We are led to suggest, in certain cases, the desirability of higher prices for resource-exporting countries. This suggestion is not new, although the basis for our arguments is quite different from that of previous ones. Moreover, our arguments lead us to suggest not only higher prices but, in some cases, ceilings for such prices as well. The recommendation is therefore not always to increase prices: It is, however, to increase them when they are too low in a precisely defined sense.

The importance c' higher commodity prices has been emphasized for many years by international organizations such as UNCTAD. The issue here has been the *stabilization* of these prices at higher ranges, since price fluctuations can be very disruptive for the producers. Commodity price stabilization schemes have become a trademark of UNCTAD and have been widely discussed in international circles. They have also been widely criticized as interfering with market adjustment processes and therefore leading to inefficiency, as well as for requiring unrealistically high and costly amounts of "buffer stocks" to avoid large fluctuations.[17] This and other related suggestions made in favor of higher commodity prices were based on voluntary agreements that challenged or ignored market behavior and the self-interest of some of the economic agents involved. In particular, these suggestions appeared to ignore the interests of the re-

[16] This model is presented fully in G. Chichilnisky, "Oil Prices, Industrial Prices and Outputs: A Simple General Equilibrium Macro Model," Columbia University Discussion Paper. This model is also discussed in G. M. Heal and G. Chichilnisky, *Oil and the International Economy* (op. cit.), and in G. Chichilnisky, G. M. Heal, and A. Sepahban, "Non-Conflicting Resource-Pricing Policies in an Interdependent World," *OPEC Review* (Spring 1983). There is a review in G. Chichilnisky, "General Equilibrium Models of International Trade in Resources," in R. McKelvey (ed.), *The Mathematics of Natural Resources,* American Mathematical Society, Providence, Rhode Island, 1985.

[17] See D. M. G. Newbery and J. E. Stiglitz, *The Theory of Commodity Price Stabilization: A Study in the Economics of Risk,* Oxford University Press, London, 1981.

source importing countries. For this and other reasons, the schemes were never quite successful, although advances were made in certain markets.[18] Eventually commodity price stabilization schemes went the way of North-South transfer policies: They were never considered realistic, gradually lost immediacy, and finally disappeared.

Our suggestion of a substantial community of interest between importers and exporters differs from all the above in that it is grounded in the analysis of the response of competitive markets to resource prices. As such it is a rather novel proposal and may have far-reaching implications. It is therefore of interest to understand exactly the framework from which it emerges: that of an industrial economy with perfectly competitive domestic markets that responds to a given world market price for a resource. This economy imports resources in exchange for industrial goods. Departing from previous analysis, the resource importing economy is not assumed here to be a small country, but rather a large one with some influence on international prices. The resource exporter fixes the world price of the resource and so is a price setter. However, the resource exporter has no control over the prices of the industrial goods that it receives in exchange for resources: These emerge from the behavior of the importer and are of course influenced by the price of the resource. Hence the exporter cannot set the terms of trade between resources and industrial goods, which is the "real" price of the resource; the exporter only sets the resource price alone, which is a "nominal" price. The competitive market response of the industrial economy then determines the price of industrial goods and hence the terms of trade or the "real" resource price. The *real price* of the resource is determined jointly by the exporter and by the free play of market forces in the importing economy.

This framework is quite different from the conventional models of monopoly in the world resource market, where it is assumed that the importer is a "small country" and that the seller sets the "real" price of the resource, that is, the terms of trade between this and the goods traded for it. Equally, it is different from a fully competitive model where the resource exporter is a small country with no influence on prices. In this model the price-setting power of the resource exporter is mediated by the market's response in the importing country, which determines a price for the industrial imports and hence the terms of trade. In our framework the resource exporter can set any "nominal" price but has to live with whatever real price is the market's response.

This seems to be an accurate representation of the positions of many resource-exporting countries, or of the positions to which they aspire.

---

[18] See Newberry and Stiglitz, op. cit.

Certainly it describes OPEC's position well: They have been able to fix, or at least influence strongly, the current dollar price of oil, but have had to accept the current dollar prices of exports with which the OECD economies have responded. These have risen sufficiently sharply since 1973 to make OPEC's gain in real oil prices a fraction of its gain in current dollar prices.[19] We are therefore concerned with comparing a short- with a medium-term effect of resource prices. In the short run the exporter fixes the dollar price, but in the medium run it must accept a market-determined "real" price for its resource. Experience indicates that these short- and medium-term prices can be significantly different.

7.4 Resource prices and the exporter

We turn now to an analysis of the reaction of the resource-exporting country to export price levels. Again it proves useful to distinguish various types of effect. This time the distinction is between the impact of a pricing policy on export revenues and on the internal economic structure of the country. These are call *revenue* and *structural effects.*[20]

The *revenue effects* are predictable. If the price increases from a very low initial level, then the total revenue from sales will rise. This hardly needs explaining. However, at very high prices, an increase will eventually reduce revenues. This is partly because high prices encourage substitution and so reduce demand (the factor use effect referred to above), and partly because they lead to a deflation of the consuming economy and so reduce demand via the wealth effect, also analyzed above.

In the intermediate price range, the revenue effects of a price change are more complex and depend on the structural characteristics of the importing economy. Precise results require technical statements, but it is certainly clear that at low prices the revenue effects of a price rise are beneficial to the exporter, and that at high prices they are harmful.

This analysis is couched in terms of the effect of a change in the *money* price of oil on the *real* revenues of the exporter, by which we mean its revenues denominated in terms of the goods that it imports. This is important, as an increase in the price of a raw material will typically lead to rises in the prices of products embodying it. These consequential price

[19] There is some dispute about the precise figures, as these depend on the index of OPEC import prices used. However, while nominal oil prices have risen by a factor of over 15, real prices have risen by a factor of at most 3. This is based on data from the IMF *International Financial Statistics Yearbook 1982,* and on private communications from the OECD.

[20] Details are in G. Chichilnisky, "Resources and North–South Trade: A Macro Analysis of Open Economies," Columbia University Discussion Paper, 1981.

changes have to be considered when evaluating alternative pricing strategies.

Next, we study the *structural effects* of a price change on the exporting country. These are more complex and have both positive and negative aspects. They depend upon the characteristics of the two trading economies. A key variable here is the degree of duality in these economies. As in earlier chapters, duality is measured essentially by the differences between the factor-intensities of the various sectors. We call an economy *dual* if it contains a very capital-intensive industrial sector and a very labor-intensive traditional sector.

7.5   Resource exports and the dual economy

Chapter 4 explored the consequences of duality for export strategies. The exporting economies also had a labor supply that was highly responsive to real wages, or else expenditure patterns leading to most wage income being spent on the exportable, a labor-intensive good. It was shown that, under these conditions, an expansion of exports may actually harm the terms of trade and the position of wage earners in the exporting economy. Exporting more could lead to lower wages and lower export revenues.

We now examine the effects on profits. They are complex, and depend on the initial export price level. From a very low initial price, an increase in the price of the exported raw material will lead to an increase in the profitability of domestic capital, and also to an increase in the use of capital. The consequences are the opposite if the initial price is high. Therefore the profitability and the employment of domestic capital increase or decrease with the export price precisely when revenues increase or decrease. The intuition behind this is rather clear: An increase in export revenues raises domestic demand for capital and leads to higher prices and employment of capital. A decrease has the opposite effect. Again, for intermediate price levels, one must turn to more detailed technical analysis.

To summarize this discussion of the impact of pricing policies on a dualistic resource-exporting country:

1. Revenues of the exporter increase when prices are increased from low levels or decreased from high levels.
2. Profitability and capital income in the exporting country increase when prices are increased from low levels or decreased from high levels.
3. Wages and wage income respond in the opposite sense to profits.

In general there may be a conflict between higher profits and higher wages in a dualistic resource-exporting economy. Profit income in general benefits from an expansion of resource exports more than wage income. However, this summary applies only to price increases from low or high initial levels, respectively. At intermediate price ranges there may be price movements that increase *both* profits and wages: The complexity of the conditions under which this occurs may explain the difficulties of policy making in dual resource-exporting economies. During the past ten years, such difficulties were evident in the major oil-exporting, middle-income developing countries such as Mexico, Nigeria, Venezuela, and Ecuador, all of which have dual economies. The evidence of these past ten years actually shows that middle-income oil-exporting countries grew about 20% less than their oil-importing peers over the 1973–83 period.[21] Furthermore, a list of the largest debtors in the world economy[22] includes several oil-exporting developing countries in the top ten places.

7.6   Resource exports and the homogeneous economy

We have dealt above with the case of a dualistic resource-exporting country from the point of view of establishing a common interest between importers and exporters. Duality is in fact the worst case. If instead the exporting economy is homogeneous, then in the situations described above real wages and profits can increase together as resource exports vary. A price increase from low initial levels will increase revenues, profits, *and* wages. In both cases, the traditional and the industrial sector expand together, a most desirable outcome for the resource-exporting economy. A decrease from high initial levels will do likewise.

We have pointed out one significant advantage of a homogeneous economy: Profit income and wage income can generate positive external ities for each other, so that they may increase simultaneously. This occurs because, in such well-integrated economies, increases in wage income lead to increases in the demand for capital-intensive products as well, and this leads to higher capital use and higher profits. Increases in capital income can likewise have a positive effect on wage income. A homogeneous, well-integrated economy therefore distributes the gains from exports more evenly than does a dual economy.

As a general proposition, a country stands to gain more from resource exports the more homogeneous are its technologies and the higher are its initial real wages. Indeed, the greatest gains accrue to a homogeneous, high-wage economy exporting resources to a dualistic, low-wage country. So an industrial economy such as Australia or Canada stands to gain from

21 The World Bank, *World Development Report, 1984.*
22 "External Debt of Developing Countries,"OECD.

an expansion of mineral or fuel exports to South America or the Far East. A South American or African country, on the other hand, is less likely to gain uniformly from expanding resource exports to North America or to Europe. Mexico, Venezuela, Ecuador, and Nigeria are cases in point.

7.7   Resource prices and the economic policies of industrial countries

We have analyzed a significant community of interests between buyers and sellers in the international markets for resources: There are price movements that will benefit buyers and also benefit sellers in terms of export revenues and capital income, though in some cases they may worsen the position of wage earners in the selling countries and require compensating policies. The next step is to analyze the factors that actually do influence price movements in these markets.

Domestic policies of importing countries may affect international resource prices to a great extent. It is well understood that an increase in demand will generally raise prices, and there is certainly evidence that economic expansion of the consuming countries has affected the levels of resource prices. What may be more surprising is that domestic policies such as interest rate policies also have a significant impact on resource prices. There are both theoretical and empirical reasons for this, based on the fact that extractive resources are economic assets and behave as such.

Extractive resources have many of the characteristics of assets such as currency holdings, stocks, and bonds. This is rather clear of gold, whose price often reflects the behavior of international currencies such as the U.S. dollar. Consequently an equilibrium in extractive resource markets is described by the same kinds of conditions as characterize equilibrium in other asset markets. One such condition is that all equivalent assets should yield their holders the same expected rate of return, for otherwise these holders would alter their portfolio. The rate of return to a good that pays no dividend is simply the rate at which its price appreciates, namely the rate of capital gains that it produces. The return to holding an extractive resource therefore depends upon the rate at which its price increases. Market equilibrium requires that this rate be related to the rates of return available on other assets such as bonds. Such rates of return are determined inter alia by interest rates. There is therefore a chain of connections running from interest rates to the rates of change of resource prices. It can be shown that whatever the market structure – competitive, imperfectly competitive, or monopolistic – there will be a positive relationship between the rate of change of resource prices and rates of interest.

This is the classic "Hotelling rule,"[23] which relates resource price movements to interest rates. It establishes that, in the long run, resource prices will follow an upward trend that is related to the general level of interest rates. Unanticipated changes in interest rates will lead to changes in this trend rate of increase and also to abrupt changes in the level of resource prices. There is an analogy here with the impact of interest rates on asset prices in general: Unanticipated changes in interest rates raise or lower the prices of assets such as stocks and bonds. The rising long-run trend of resource prices simply reflects their increasing scarcity, as the remaining stock becomes smaller.[24]

This prediction was considered surprising when it was first introduced fifty years ago. It has since then received extensive empirical scrutiny, from which it has emerged essentially unscathed and is now a classic result in the economics of extractive resources.[25]

From the point of view of understanding the international economic system, the relevant point is that the prices of extractive resources are not exogenous to domestic policies of the industrial countries. Via the logic of the Hotelling rule, they are strongly influenced by their interest rate policies. In the medium run, higher interest rates lead to higher rates of increase of resource prices, at least if the logic of the market prevails.

The domestic policies pursued by the industrial countries influence the prices that they face in resource markets, so that the level of these prices cannot be attributed solely to the actions of the sellers. They are indeed amenable to policy actions on the part of the buyers.

7.8   Community of interest in resource markets

The various strands of arguments in this chapter can now be pulled together to make a whole. Two important points emerge. One is that the pricing of internationally traded resources need not always be a source of

---

[23] This analysis was first developed in the classical paper by Harold Hotelling, "The Economics of Exhaustible Resources," *Journal of Political Economy* 39 (1931), 137–75. The implications of this dynamic approach for the long-run outcome of cooperative pricing policies is studied in Chichilnisky, Heal, and Sepahban, "Non-Conflicting Resource-Pricing Policies in an Interdependent World"(op. cit.) and in Heal and Chichilnisky, *Oil in the International Economy* (op. cit.).

[24] For a detailed discussion, see Heal and Chichilnisky, *Oil in the International Economy* (op. cit.).

[25] G. M. Heal and M. Barrow, "Metal Price Movements and Interest Rates," *Review of Economic Studies* (1981) and "Empirical Investigation of Mineral Price Movements," *Economic Letters* 7(1) (1981), 95–103.

North–South conflict. There are common interests that, if well understood, could lead to prices attractive to both sides of the market. Crucial
here is the recognition that very low or very high prices may be to no-
body's benefit. We argued that both may lead to welfare losses; they may
also lead to instability. Low prices lead with a lag to an expanded and
inelastic demand for resources, and thus to an upward pressure on
prices.[26] The commodity price boom of the early 1970s can be seen in part
as a demand response to a long period (since 1950) of low prices.

Similarly, high prices lead eventually to a depressed market, one in
which substitutes for the resource are increasingly utilized and demand
for them becomes more elastic. They thus lead to a "buyer's" market, as is
currently the case with oil.

It was noted that both exporters and importers exercise influence over
price movements. The precise nature of the relationship between economic policies in the consuming countries and international price movements can be set out in the detail needed for policy analysis in each
country; the level of complexity should not exceed current practice. The
general implication of these observations is once again that national and
international economic issues are intimately linked, so that neither can be
considered in isolation.

National and international policies must be formulated consistently.
Understanding common interests between exporters and importers
should facilitate this task. Indeed the foregoing analysis makes clear the
main sources of common interests, and more technical discussion can set
out in detail the precise parameters. Numerical evaluation of the effects
discussed can disclose the regimes within which coordinated policies
would be mutually beneficial for a variety of extractive resources. These
resources would have to be economically important inputs, either indi-
vidually, as in the case of oil, or in groups that can naturally be considered
together, as in the case of nonferrous, nonprecious metals. Otherwise the
impacts of their price changes would not be significant enough to produce
the wealth, factor-use, and recycling effects necessary to make cooperative
pricing policies possible.

---

[26] For example, the International Institute for Applied System Analysis (IIASA) in its
publication *Options,* Autumn 1982, comments on "the fear that today's oil glut masks the
threat to tomorrow's energy users."

PART III

Summary

CHAPTER 8

The evolving world economy

We have touched upon a wide range of issues: on protectionism and managed trade, on recent macroeconomic development linked with new technologies, and on North–South interdependence via international financial markets, export strategies, arms trade, and resource pricing. Although the scope is broad, there have been a number of recurrent themes. In fact, there is a single theme that emerges strongly: that attention must be paid to domestic economic structures in order to ascertain the impact of international policies. Reciprocally, national economic policy must be responsive to the rapidly changing world economy.

Two particular features emerge from our analysis. One is economies of scale arising from new technologies in industrial countries. Another is the importance of technological dualism and labor supply conditions in determining domestic responses to export policies in developing countries. A consequence of these features is that certain conventional and widely adopted policies often have results that are quite the contrary of those intended. Examples are transfer policies and export promotion based on labor-intensive products in developing countries. Alternative policies are required in such cases, policies based on the strengthening of domestic markets. We have suggested general guidelines.

Economies of scale are reshaping the economic behavior of the industrial countries. In particular, they affect the stability of their markets, the possibility of smooth structural change, and the prerequisites of mutually beneficial and balanced international trade. Increasing returns are an important link between the emergence of stagflation and growth without inflation and the problems connected with trade imbalances and structural change at the international level.

With increasing returns, restrictive monetary policies are less efficient in controlling inflation and may impose unacceptable efficiency losses in terms of plant closures and unemployment. Equally the traditional presumptions that favor across-the-board liberalization of international trade are no longer operative: Sector-specific policies may be required. We suggest a framework for domestic policies and for the management of trade for economies with increasing returns to scale.

Links between factor and goods markets in developing countries were

105

singled out as an important feature of their economies, due to the fact that income changes have serious effects on demand at lower levels of income. If substantial, these links may reverse the conventional wisdom about the effects of international markets on domestic markets: The expansion of the export sector may lead to a contraction rather than to an expansion in the domestic sector. An increase in the exports of primary or labor-intensive commodities, even if this is due to an expansion in international demand, can lower the earnings of those producing them. This occurs precisely where demand responses to income changes are large and supply responses are sluggish. We have discussed policies that could reverse this negative connection between the export sector and the domestic sector.

Similar issues arise with respect to resources prices: The effects of these on welfare in the consuming and producing countries depend on the relative magnitudes of the wealth and factor-use effects. We have argued, and this is an argument backed by empirical evidence,[1] that circumstances where links between factor and goods markets are very powerful are in fact likely to arise frequently in markets of importance to developing countries. These circumstances are abundant labor, dual technologies, labor-intensive exports that are domestically consumed, or exports of raw materials and resources.

We have argued that the level of interdependence in the world economy has increased very significantly. We discussed the impact of resource prices on international financial flows, including the loans that recycled OPEC revenues into loans for the rapidly growing developing countries. These loans made the borrowing countries particularly vulnerable to changes in domestic monetary policies in the industrial countries. Reciprocally, they made the banking system in the industrial countries vulnerable to the policies of lending countries that affect their ability to service those loans. In any case, the evidence suggested that the developing countries have had a significantly higher level of growth and of investment than the industrial countries over the past twelve years, although their growth has slowed down in the past three years. Despite the high oil prices during this thirteen-year period, oil-importing, middle-income countries grew more than their oil-exporting[2] counterparts. Both industrial and developing countries face a challenging and volatile international environment. There is a need to revise the international decision-making institutions to accommodate the new conditions.

Consider the domestic macroeconomic policies of the industrial market economies, whose sluggish performance in the late 1970s and early

---

[1] For empirical studies, see Chapter 4.
[2] See, for example, *World Development Report 1984, World Bank,* Washington, D.C.

1980s adversely affected export earnings of many developing countries. We argued here for selective expansionary fiscal and monetary policies. Clearly, the expansion must be directed toward those sectors with the greatest potential for cost reductions from scale economies. However, there is a danger that an attempt at rapid expansion of output in these sector will cause bottlenecks in the markets for labor and other inputs, with inflationary consequences. Because of this, the directed expansion would have to be associated with policies to encourage the availability of appropriate inputs to these sectors. These might involve subsidies to the retraining of labor and to labor mobility, and also to related capital expenditures. It is important to note that there are several possible policy responses to the need for structural change. A positive response would be that outlined above: Encourage the sectors with potential and also expedite reallocations from sectors with lower, to those with higher, potential.[3] A negative response would be to subsidize or protect declining sectors so as to keep them extant.[4] If the underlying loss of competitiveness in such sectors is permanent, then this latter response can only lead to a cycle of declining efficiency and of rising subsidies. Public resources are in general much more productive when spent facilitating the growth of emerging industries with potential for cost reductions, and relocating labor correspondingly, than when spent attempting to maintain an existing but declining industrial base. Short-run social costs must, however, be integrated into this equation.

Finally, we consider the relationship of developing countries with the international market. Here, one of the main thrusts of our analysis has been to warn against the dangers of excessive dependence on international markets as an engine of growth, especially with respect to traditional exports. The outcome of participation in such markets is extremely sensitive not only to price fluctuations and to protectionism in the industrial countries, but also to domestic market and technological structures.

In particular, the importance of the links between factor and goods markets has already been mentioned. When these links are substantial – and there are reasons to believe that, in dual economies with abundant labor, they are – then involvement in international markets for primary commodities can lead to a country becoming trapped in a self-reinforcing position of domestic poverty, dependence, and stagnation. An excessively international orientation leads to dependence on imports and to a vulnerability to balance-of-payments deficits during cyclical downswings. Such

---

[3] Such policies have been pursued in connection with coal and steel sectors in the European Economic Community.
[4] Policies toward textile industries in Europe and the United States exemplify this approach.

payments deficits lead to pressures from international organizations for restrictive domestic policies and for devaluations, both with a view to emphasizing the promotion of exports. These may increase further the international orientation of the economy and undermine further its growth and its distribution of income. Ultimately, developing countries would fulfill essentially a service role in the international economy, as suppliers of cheap exports to the industrial countries.

Stronger domestic markets, which are associated with higher agricultural productivity and with more integrated and productive technological structures in the developing countries, may lead to gains from an expansion of exports. In this case, increased participation in international markets for labor-intensive goods or for primary commodities may be beneficial to the exporter. This suggests two policy conclusions.

One is that involvement in international primary commodity markets should be undertaken only after a careful review of domestic economic conditions. These structures are not unchangeable and could be subject to influence by suitable policy measures in the labor market and in the field of choice of productive technique, both selected with a view to strengthening domestic markets. The other suggestion to emerge clearly is that there may be substantial advantages to exporting goods that are skill- or capital-intensive rather than very labor-intensive, as potentially harmful linkages are less likely to arise with the former than with the latter. There may also be substantial gains for the South from a careful choice of trading partners and from participation in the very dynamic South–South trade, which tends to lead to more capital-intensive exports than North–South trade.[5]

The structure of domestic markets is an important determinant of the outcome of international trade policies. The strengthening of domestic markets, by reducing technological dualism and the elasticity of labor supplies and by improving labor productivity in the traditional sector, is a valuable preliminary to greater involvement in international markets. The traditional view of cheap labor as the main relative advantage of developing countries is therefore not a good basis for the formulation of economic strategies. Countries that have pursued successful export-led growth policies over the past decade include Japan, Korea, Germany (FRG), Taiwan, and Singapore. These countries expanded their exports, and grew very rapidly. All of these exporters had highly educated, productive labor and strong, thriving domestic markets. Agricultural productivity in all of them is relatively high; in Korea and Taiwan it grew at an

---

[5] Chapter 4 discusses the emergence of South–South trade as the most dynamic segment of the world economy.

unprecedented rate since the 1950s due to energetic agricultural policies based on previous land reform. On these counts, these exporters compare very favorably with the Latin American and African countries, which neglected domestic markets and agricultural productivity and followed unsuccessful export-promotion policies, often based on the abundant labor provided by mass poverty.

Widespread poverty is not a relative advantage but a weakness. When participating in international markets, a country with a better bargaining position is one where the local population is viewed as prospective customers, rather than only as a source of cheap labor. A more integrated approach is required. The local population must be viewed as belonging to both sides of the market: as consumers (demand) as well as inputs (supply). This emphasizes the practical importance of better distributions of income.

A similar point can be made at the international level. The increased interdependence between the North and the South in recent years has taught us the practical importance of a more integrated approach to international relations and indeed to international economics. The developing countries should not be viewed, or view themselves, only as a source of inexpensive inputs such as energy or labor-intensive products. They are increasingly a relevant part of the international demand for goods and services, and a powerful source of competition in many international markets where skill and enterprise are required. The statistical evidence suggests that they are an important part of the OECD export market and are increasingly trading with each other. Their changing role in the world economy is transforming them from suppliers of cheap labor into competitors and valuable consumers of the industrial countries. This progress is certainly not uniform, nor is it without temporary drawbacks and fluctuations, such as the present international financial difficulties. However, much conflict and pain could be avoided by adopting policies that use rather than fight these trends in the evolving world economy.

PART IV

Theoretical background

Chapters 9–12 contain analytical foundations for some of the arguments used in the previous three parts of the book. This part complements the earlier chapters and is addressed to readers with an interest in economic theory.

Our main theoretical foundations are provided by the Arrow–Debreu general equilibrium model, as presented, for example, by Arrow and Hahn.* This is the standard model for analyzing a market economy and the interaction among its various sectors. These interactions, which are the essence of general equilibrium theory, drive many of our conclusions, particularly those of Chapters 4–7.

The basic general equilibrium framework is amply developed in the literature, so we need not repeat it here. However, there are two recent advances in general equilibrium theory that we use extensively and that are available only in technical journals. The purpose of Part IV is to make these developments accessible to the reader.

One of these developments concerns economies with increasing returns to scale in production. The other concerns North–South trade and the study of the effects of domestic economic structures on the gains and losses from such trade. We are not aiming to give a rigorous presentation, but to indicate the basic elements of the analysis and provide an intuitive grasp of how the main results emerge. Full details can always be found in the technical references given.

*K. J. Arrow and F. H. Hahn. *General Competitive Analysis.* Holden-Day, Oakland, CA, 1971.

CHAPTER 9

Adjustment, stability, and returns to scale

Chapter 2 discussed the macroeconomic stability of modern industrial economies in which substantial sectors are characterized by economies of scale in production. A related analysis appeared in our discussion of protectionism and managed trade in Chapter 3. In this chapter we outline the formal arguments that lie behind these discussions.[1]

9.1 The model

Our aim is to study how prices, output levels, profits, and productivity move over time in an economy with increasing returns to scale. We use a straightforward framework: Prices are assumed to change in response to the difference between demand and supply, and supply is assumed to respond to profits, that is, to the difference between price and cost. Prices rise with excess demand, output rises with profits, and vice versa: When supply exceeds demand, prices fall, and when average cost exceeds price, output falls. This is the classical adjustment process discussed by Walras,[2] who argued for "le loi de l'offre et de la demande" – the law of supply and demand, according to which prices move with the difference between supply and demand – and for "le loi de revient," according to which production moves in the direction that increases profits.

Figure 9.1 presents a conventional picture: The curve AA shows how average cost $c(q)$ changes with output q, which is measured horizontally. Price is measured vertically, and the curve BB shows how demand $D(p)$ varies with the price. The demand curve, of course, slopes down – demand falls as price rises – and in this particular case the average cost curve slopes up, showing the average cost of production rising with output: There are diminishing returns to scale or diseconomies of scale in productions. Large-scale production is less efficient and has higher costs per unit of output than small-scale.

[1] For a detailed algebraic analysis this reader is referred to G. M. Heal, "Macrodynamics and Returns to Scale," *Economic Journal*, 96 (March 1986), 191–8 and "Stable Disequilibrium Prices: Macroeconomics and Increasing Returns," Columbia Business School Research Working Paper no. 533A, 1983.
[2] Walras, L. (1954), *Elements of Pure Economics*, R. Irwin.

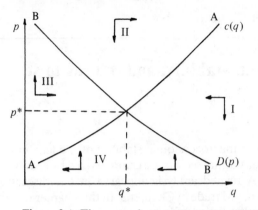

Figure 9.1. The system's movement depends upon the region.

We argued in earlier chapters that in this case the economy has certain natural robustness or stability properties. The argument is straightforward. Consider an equilibrium state of the economy characterized by certain firm and sectoral output levels. Suppose that this is disturbed, leading to a contraction of one unit's output. Then as its output falls, its average costs will also fall, improving its competitive position. This leads to higher demand for its products and tends to restore the initial configuration.

9.2   Formal analysis

Figure 9.1 can be used to confirm these intuitive arguments. The adjustment process that we have in mind can be written as

$$\frac{dp}{dt} = K_1(D(p) - q), \quad K_1 > 0, \tag{9.1}$$

that is, price changes at a rate proportional to the difference between demand $D(p)$, which depends on price, and output q. Then output changes according to

$$\frac{dq}{dt} = K_2(p - c(q)), \quad K_2 > 0, \tag{9.2}$$

so that output expands at a rate proportional to the difference between price p and average cost $c(q)$, which depends upon output q. In equations (9.1) and (9.2), K_1 and K_2 are positive constants of proportionality.

Figure 9.1 has been divided into four regions, depending on the posi-

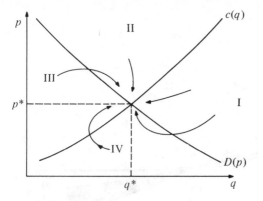

Figure 9.2. With diminishing returns there is a stable equilibrium.

tion in relation to the curves $D(p)$ and $c(q)$. Consider first region I, above $D(p)$ and below $c(q)$. This region consists of points (q, p), where price is less than cost, that is, $p < c(q)$. Equation (9.2) tells us that, when price is less than cost, output q must be falling at these points. The points (q, p) in region I also satisfy $q > D(p)$, that is, output exceeds demand, so that from (9.1), price is falling. Hence in region I, we conclude that the system must be moving down and to the left: Both q and p will be falling.

As the system moves down and to the left from region I, it meets the curve $D(p)$. On this curve, $q = D(p)$, demand exactly equals output, and from equation (9.1), price is constant. So on the curve $q = D(p)$, only output is changing: As we are still below $c(q)$, price is less than cost and output is still falling, so that movement is horizontally to the left.

This leads into region IV, which consists of points (q, p) where price is less than cost, $p < c(p)$, so that output is falling; but now output falls short of demand, $q < D(p)$, so that price is rising. Hence the system's movement is now up and to the left.

A similar analysis carried out for the other regions III and II will confirm that, from any initial combination of price and output, the system will move along the kinds of trajectory shown in Figure 9.2 and toward the point (q^*, p^*), which is the intersection of the demand and cost curves. Here demand equals supply and price equals average cost, and in the case of rising average costs – diminishing returns – this represents a stable configuration.

Figure 9.3 shows a similar analysis, but for the case when there are substantially increasing returns in production, so that average cost falls with output and falls rapidly enough to cut the demand curve $D(p)$ from

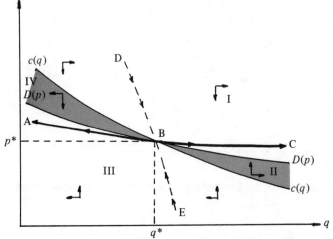

Figure 9.3. Directions of motion by region with increasing returns.

above. There are again four regions, or four types of (q, p) pair, giving rise to different types of motion. In region I, we have (q, p) such that price exceeds cost, $p > c(q)$, and output exceeds demand, $q > D(p)$. Hence in this region output is rising and the price falling. In region II, we still have $p > c(q)$, price exceeding cost, so output still rises. But now $q < D(p)$, demand exceeds supply, so that price rises.

A similar analysis can be conducted for the other regions, with the results shown. Note also that, on the curve $q = D(p)$, demand equals supply and so price is constant. Only output changes: To the right of the intersection of the demand and cost curves it rises, and to the left it falls. Similarly, on the curve $c(q) = p$, price equals cost and so output is constant: Only price changes.

Putting together the directions of movement shown, it is clear that:

1. A path starting in region II must move into I.
2. A path starting in region IV must move into III.
3. A path starting in I may move into IV or stay in I.
4. A path starting in III may move into II or stay in III.

The trajectories of Figure 9.4 assemble these observations into an overall pattern of motion. There is a curve ABC with the property that, from almost any initial (q, p) pair, the system converges toward this curve. The only exceptions are points on the curve DBE, from which the system moves to (q^*, p^*), the intersection of the demand and cost curves. Effectively, then, the system moves in the long run to one of the two branches of

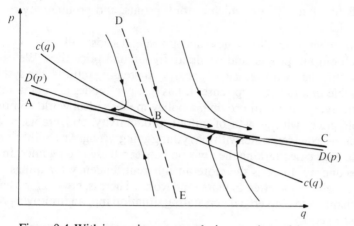

Figure 9.4. With increasing returns, the intersections of the two curves is an unstable equilibrium, and prices and outputs concentrate around ABC.

the curve ABC: either the branch moving to the right (BC) if it is initially to the right of DBE, or the branch BA otherwise.

What are the economic conclusions to be extracted from this? With diminishing returns – rising average costs – the intersection of the demand and cost curves, where supply equals demand and price equals cost, is a stable equilibrium of the system: After any disturbance, the system will return to it. However, with returns increasing sharply enough that the cost curve cuts the demand curve from above, this is no longer the case. Of course, the intersection of the two curves still represents a point where demand and supply are equal and price equals cost, so that there is no tendency for price or output to change. It is, in other words, still an equilibrium: It is not, however, a *stable* equilibrium. If the system is displaced from this equilibrium, it will not return toward it: The displacement will cumulate and evolve into a movement along BA or BC. This certainly confirms the original intuition that, with economies of scale, the system can become unstable.

One can say rather more than this. In the case of Figure 9.4, any displacement from the equilibrium at the intersection of the demand and cost curves will lead to one of two outcomes. One possibility is that the system will move along BC, with output rising and price falling. It is easy to see that although price is falling, profits are rising, because *c(q)* slopes down more than BC, so that cost is falling faster than price. Costs, of course, are falling because of economies of scale, which lead to greater productivity. So one possibility is that a displacement from equilibrium leads to a path BC on which output, profits, and productivity rise and price falls.

The other possibility is the exact opposite: It leads to the path BA, along which output, profits, and productivity fall and price rises. We can see from this that, with sufficiently sharply increasing returns, the system is unstable in a rather deep sense. It has just two modes of operation: one where everything is improving, a policy maker's ideal world combining stable prices with growth of output, productivity, and profits; and the other the exact opposite, with everything going wrong. An equilibrium is a knife-edge case marking the division between these two regimes. In such an economy, there is therefore an inherent tendency for things to get either better and better, or worse and worse. There is, however, no natural mechanism to convert a deteriorating situation into an improving one – or vice versa.

9.3   Interpretation

The model discussed so far has obviously been very simple: We have deliberately kept it that way, to make it tractable. This, of course, raises questions about what precisely it is supposed to represent. The most straightforward interpretation is as an aggregative model of a sector, or indeed of a whole economy, in the spirit of the one-sector growth models used for studying long-run dynamics or optimal accumulation paths. The model can easily be extended to deal with the dynamics of several competing firms within a sector, but in this case a purely graphical treatment is no longer possible.

In its aggregative interpretation, the model produces results that are similar to those reached by other authors on a rather different basis and consistent with the number of widely noted stylized facts. The analogous results are those of the "vicious/virtuous-circle" models, which see the aggregative macroeconomic performance of a model as subject to strong positive feedbacks that make both successes and failures self-reinforcing.[3] The stylized facts are that countries (or sectors within a country) with above-average rates of output growth also have above-average rates of productivity growth and below-average rates of price increase. Conversely, countries or sectors with below-average rates of output growth tend to do poorly in terms of productivity growth and price stability.[4]

[3] W. Beckerman and associates, *The British Economy in 1975*, Cambridge University Press, 1965. See also F. Blackaby (ed.) *De-Industrialization*, National Institute and Heinneman, London, 1979

[4] See, for example, H. Houlthaker, "Growth and Inflation: Analysis by Industry," *Brookings Papers on Economic Activity* 1(1979), 240–57 and N. Kaldor, *The Causes of the Slow Rate of Growth of the U.K. Economy*, Cambridge University Press, 1967.

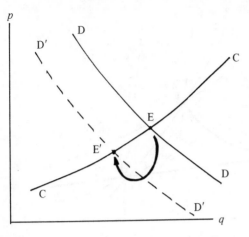

Figure 9.5. Smooth response to structural change with diminishing returns.

Clearly this is consistent with countries or sectors tending to concentrate around the curves BC or BA in Figure 9.4.

9.4   Structural change

We have so far developed the implications of the simple dynamic model set out above for macroeconomic stability. It also has implications for the possibility of smooth structural change. Structural change is not an easy concept to define: We shall take it to mean a significant change in an economy's price and output configuration resulting from a shift in its underlying demand and cost structures. So in terms of our earlier diagrams, structural change corresponds to a shift in demand or cost curves in such a way as to lead to a significant change in their intersection and so in the equilibrium of the economy. We can then say that structural change will be achieved smoothly if, by following the adjustment process discussed above, the economy adjusts continuously from the old to the new equilibrium in response to a change in its underlying parameters.

In the case of diminishing returns to scale shown in Figure 9.2, this will certainly happen. Figure 9.5 portrays an economy originally at the intersection E of cost curve CC and demand curve DD, where the demand curve has shifted downwards to D'D' with a new intersection E'. There may be some overshooting as prices and outputs adjust to their new equilibrium values, but these values will eventually be reached.

Contrast this with Figure 9.6, which shows what happens if there is a

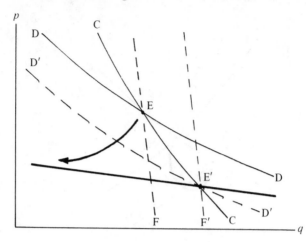

Figure 9.6. Unstable response to structural change with increasing returns.

downward shift of the demand curve in the case of significantly increasing returns, the case shown in Figures 9.3 and 9.4. Initially there was an unstable equilibrium at E: The drop in demand moves this to E', with higher output and lower prices. If the economy were initially at or near E, then the movement of the demand curve to D'D' would cause it to start moving along a trajectory down and to the left, as shown in Figure 9.6. This, of course, corresponds to a region IV trajectory in Figure 9.3 so, instead of moving toward the new equilibrium, the economy will move cumulatively away from it, in an unfavorable direction. More generally, the effect of the downward shift in demand is the following. Initially, any initial point to the left of EF sends the economy off along a "bad" path: After the change, the set of initial points giving rise to "bad" paths has been enlarged to include anything to the left of E'F'. So if the economy was initially between EF and E'F' on a "good" path, the structural shift would change its behavior and send it off along a path of falling output, profits, and productivity.

The general point here is that if an economy behaves in an unstable fashion, then a change in its underlying parameters – a structural change – can lead to a very abrupt change in its behavior. The consequences of a change in the economic environment can be very great, as can the costs. This can naturally lead to a strong desire to preserve the status quo.

There is another aspect of this same phenomenon that reinforces these conclusions: With economies of scale in production, firms or industries that are declining will contract suddenly and discontinuously, rather than

Price, average cost

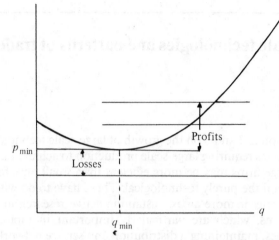

Figure 9.7. This firm will close down once price is less than p_{min}.

smoothly. There will come a point in their decline where they must shed a substantial amount of labor at once: Their decline will not be characterized by a gradual reduction of their labor force.

The reason for this is that economies of scale imply a minimum efficient scale of operation – a scale below which a firm cannot compete effectively and remain profitable. For a firm with a single output, this is the scale of operation associated with first attaining the minimum point of its average cost curve, the output level denoted q_{min} in Figure 9.7. For such a firm, as the market price drops toward the level at which it equals minimum average cost (the price p_{min} in Figure 9.7) output and employment will fall smoothly. However, once price is less than p_{min}, there is no scale of operation at which costs can be covered: The firm will eventually close down, shedding its entire remaining labor force in the process. With diminishing returns in production, however, the average cost curve would be upward-sloping over its entire range, so that a decline in market prices would simply lead to a continuous decline in output and employment. Policy makers are likely to find this continuous process easier to adjust to than the sudden jumps in unemployment caused by the contraction of increasing returns firms. With increasing returns, the adjustment process is more difficult and disruptive.

CHAPTER 10

Large-scale technologies and patterns of trade

10.1 Introduction

We remarked in Chapters 2 and 3 on the growth of large-scale technologies, that is, technologies requiring large-scale production to achieve efficiency. However, large firms may be more efficient than small ones for reasons that go beyond the purely technological. These have to do with superior abilities in one or more areas: sustaining active research and development programs, which are particularly important in rapidly changing product lines; maintaining a distribution and service network, which is important for consumer durables; and, sometimes, arranging access to financial markets.

This chapter develops the implications of economies of scale – arising for whatever reason – for the organization of international trade. In particular, we substantiate two assertions made in Chapter 3. One was that there may be no prices at which international markets clear. The other was that one can naturally develop from this framework an approach to the analysis of managed trade.[1]

10.2 Nonexistence of market-clearing prices

In economies with increasing returns there may be no prices at which markets clear – it may not be possible to balance supply and demand. Furthermore, the economy may actually tend to stabilize around a non-market-clearing position. This leads to a stable configuration in which markets, however, do not clear. We call this a "stable disequilibrium."

This point is illustrated by reference to an economy where two price-taking firms produce a single output from a single input. One firm produces under traditional conditions of diminishing returns to scale. The other has increasing returns at low production levels but also shows eventually diminishing returns above a certain level. So one firm has a technol-

---

[1] The analysis in this chapter follows that in G. Chichilnisky, "Trade with Increasing Returns," Working Paper, Economics Department, Columbia University, 1983; G. M. Heal, "Stable Disequilibrium Prices," Working Paper, Columbia Business School, 1983; and G. M. Heal and G. Chichilnisky, "Trade Policies with Increasing Returns," Working Paper, Woodrow Wilson School, Princeton University, 1983.

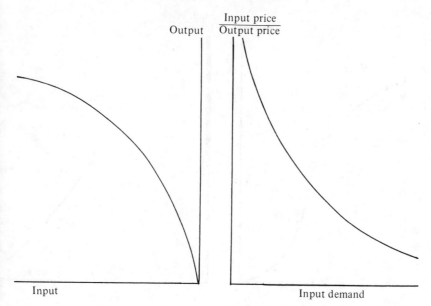

Figure 10.1. Production function and input demand with diminishing returns.

ogy adapted to small-scale operation, and the other has a large-scale technology. Their production functions are shown in Figures 10.1 and 10.2 respectively.

Figures 10.1 and 10.2 also show the quantities of the input demanded by these firms at different ratios of input to output prices. For the diminishing returns firm, input demand falls continuously as input price rises. For the increasing-returns firm, however, matters are more complex. If the input price is very low relative to the output price, then an increase leads to a continuous drop in demand; but once the price reaches p^*, the demand drops discontinuously to zero. The price ratio p^* corresponds to the slope of the line through the origin just tangent to the production frontier, which is indicated on the left-hand panel of Figure 10.2. At the price ratio represented by the slope of this line, profits are zero. At smaller levels of output, therefore, profits would be negative.

Figure 10.3 makes the same point, but in terms of the average cost curve. As the firm has increasing and then diminishing returns to scale, this average cost curve is U-shaped, with a minimum average cost c^* at a positive output level q^*. Marginal and average costs are equal at q^*. For any price $p > c^*$, this firm will produce where price equals marginal cost; that is, a price such as p_1 induces an output level such as q_1. As price falls, the firm's profit-maximizing output falls toward q^*, but once $p < c^*$,

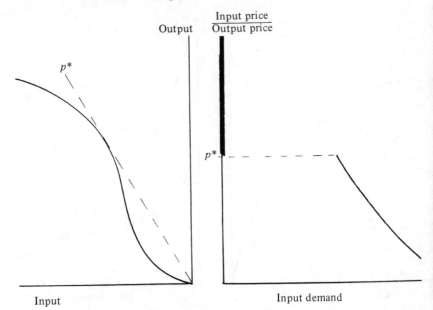

Figure 10.2. Production function and input demand with increasing then diminishing returns.

producing where price equals marginal cost will lead to a loss because marginal cost is less than average cost. For prices below c^* the firm does better to close down and produce nothing.

As the output price drops below c^*, the firm's input demand drops abruptly to zero. It is this discontinuous drop in input demand, applied in particular to the labor market, that we emphasized in the context of the difficulty of obtaining smooth adjustment to changing circumstances with economies of scale. As it is only the relative price of input to output that affect the firm, the output price falling below a critical level is equivalent to the input price rising above a critical level.

If we sum horizontally the two input demand curves shown in Figures 10.1 and 10.2, the result is that in Figure 10.4: It is a normal downward-sloping demand curve, except for the discontinuity at p^*. Raising the number of increasing-returns firms would lead to more discontinuities. Figure 10.4 also shows an increasing input supply curve of a conventional type. In the case shown, the configurations of supply and demand responses are such that at no price will demand equal supply: For $p > p^*$, supply exceeds demand, and vice versa. So there is no price at which the market clears: competitive, profit-maximizing behavior can not be relied on to equate supply and demand.

Marginal cost
Average cost
Price of output

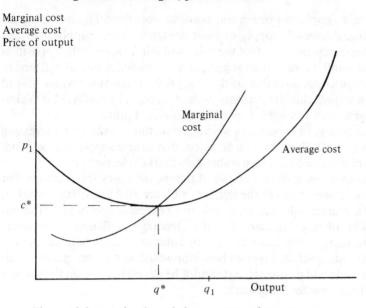

Figure 10.3. As price drops below c, output drops to zero.

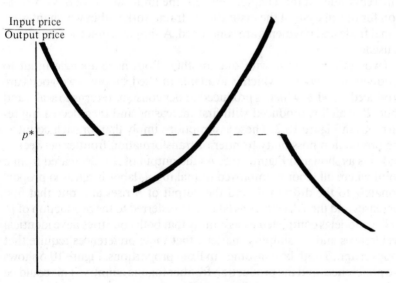

Figure 10.4. Input supply and demand curves for an economy with increasing returns.

Another simple but important point to note from Figure 10.4 is the following. Above p^*, supply exceeds demand: Excess supply naturally tends to depress price, so that the price will fall. Below p^*, the opposite is true: Demand is greater than supply, and unsatisfied demands will tend to drive the price up. So in this market, the price will tend to gravitate toward p^*, even though this is not a market-clearing price. Formally, p^* is Walrasian-stable even though it is not an equilibrium price.

In summary, in economies where production occurs with increasing returns to scale, there may be no prices that equate supply and demand; furthermore, there may be a stable non-market-clearing price.

This observation has a number of significant policy implications. For example, if one thinks of the market in Figure 10.4 as the labor market, then this market will switch abruptly from excess supply of labor (unemployment) to excess demand for labor, leading to inflation. At no intermediate stage is the labor market in balance or near balance. At the international level, this type of behavior would lead to structural imbalance in trade and payments that cannot be eliminated within the normal competitive market framework.

10.3   Persistent disequilibrium in international markets

The remainder of this chapter develops the implications of our observation for the analysis of the institutional framework within which international trade and payments are conducted. A simple geometric framework is used.

Two countries trade with one another. Both have a single input to production – labor – which is available in fixed supply. Two goods are produced: good A, which is produced under constant returns to scale, and good B, which is produced with first increasing and then decreasing returns, as in Figure 10.2. These assumptions imply that for each country, the production possibility frontier or transformation frontier between A and B is as shown in Figure 10.5. As the output of A is decreased from a point where all labor is employed in making A, labor is released proportionately to the drop in A, and the output of B rises at a rate that first increases and then decreases as labor is transferred to the production of B.

The model is completed by assuming that both countries have identical preferences and, to simplify matters, that these preferences require that goods A and B both be consumed in fixed proportions. Figure 10.6 shows the preferences and the production frontier for one country. This could be either country, as they are assumed to be the same.

Consumer preferences are such that strictly positive amounts of both goods will always be consumed and, of course, consumed in the propor-

Output of B

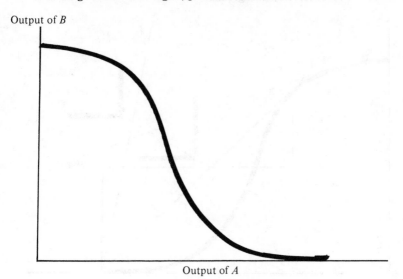

Output of A

Figure 10.5. The transformation frontier between A and B.

B

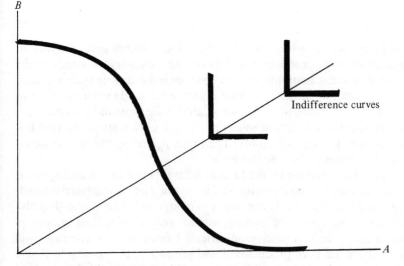

Indifference curves

A

Figure 10.6. Preferences and the production frontier.

tions indicated by the preferences. This gives us information about possible equilibrium prices in the world economy.

There are two internationally traded goods, A and B. In equilibrium, their prices must be the same in both countries: Call these prices p_A and p_B. Each country has a domestic labor supply, which under competitive

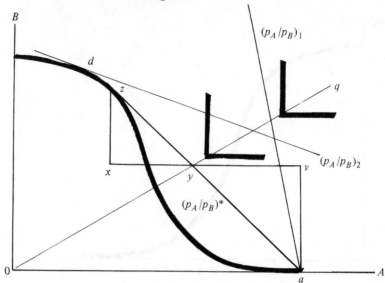

Figure 10.7. The response of production to the output price ratio.

conditions is paid a wage equal to the value of its marginal product. In each country, the productivity of labor in the A industry is constant by the constant-returns assumptions. The constant is the same in both countries because technologies are the same. As there is a single world price for A, the value of the marginal product of labor is the same in both countries; that is, there is a common wage rate. To simplify matters, we take this common wage rate to be unity. The prices p_A and p_B can now be interpreted as prices relative to labor.

Figure 10.7 investigates the effect of different values for p_A and p_B on the combination of A and B produced. The mix of A and B produced depends only on the ratio p_A/p_B. When this ratio is large, lines showing A-B combinations giving a constant level of profit are very steep, such as $(p_A/p_B)_1$ in the diagram. In this case, profit-oriented firms in both countries will specialize entirely in producing A and produce at the point a in Figure 10.7. Obviously, this cannot lead to a world market equilibrium as there will be unsatisfied demand for B.

Suppose, on the other hand, that the ratio p_A/p_B is rather low, giving, for example, the constant-profit lines labeled $(p_A/p_B)_2$ in Figure 10.7. Then in both countries profit-maximizing firms will produce at point d, where they reach the highest isoprofit line and where the marginal rate of transformation between A and B is equal to the ratio of their prices. In this case,

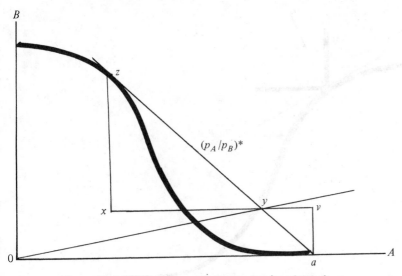

Figure 10.8. Trade does not balance at prices (p_A/p_B).

the mix of A and B produced involves a higher proportion of B than consumers wish to consume, and there will be an excess supply of B.

The only prices that could possibly clear the market are those shown as $(p_A/p_B)^*$, which produce a constant-profit line tangent to the production frontier both at a and at z. This means that both points are equally profitable and are jointly the profit-maximizing points. Hence we could suppose that one country produces at a, with A its only output, and the other produces a mix of A and B at z. Clearly any line steeper than $(p_A/p_B)^*$ will lead both countries to specialize at a, with no output of B, and any line less steep will lead both to produce at points such as d, with an excess supply of B relative to demands.

The next step, then, is to check whether production at a and at z will lead to balanced trade. Call the country that produces at a country I, and the other, country II. Both countries will have the same budget line, the line az, and both will wish to consume at y, where an indifference curve is tangent to the budget line. So country I will wish to import av of B and export vy of A; country II will wish to import xy of A and export xz of B. International markets will only clear if I's exports of A equal II's imports, $vy = xy$, and II's exports of B equal A's imports, $zx = va$.

Figure 10.7 makes it clear that these equalities will not generally hold: They will in fact only hold if the ray $0q$, the expansion path of the preferences, bisects the line az. Figure 10.8 shows a situation where this is clearly not the case: Country I wants to import va of B, whereas country II wants

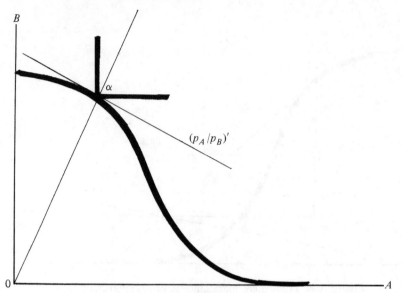

Figure 10.9. Markets clear but there is no trade.

to export the much larger quantity xz. There is a similar imbalance in the A market: Country I wishes to export vy, and II to import xy.

Similar examples can also be constructed with more general preferences that allow substitution in consumption. The difficulties in finding market-clearing prices arise on the supply side, not on the demand side. Output does not respond continuously to prices, although demand does. With diminishing returns, however, both respond continuously, and market clearing can usually be achieved.

These diagrams show that, with profit-maximizing price-taking producers, scale economies in production may make it impossible to balance international trade. Trade imbalance may be built into the structure of the international economy. Whether or not this is so depends on both preferences and production technologies. Figure 10.9 shows a case where consumers demand a combination of A and B that is relatively intensive in B. In this case, production in each country can occur at α, with market prices $(p_A/p_B)'$. All markets will clear, though each country will meet its own needs fully so that there will be no international trade.

It is interesting to note that, in Figure 10.8, although the prices $(p_A/p_B)^*$ are not market-clearing or equilibrium prices, they are Walrasian-stable: If prices respond in the usual Walrasian fashion to excess demands and supplies, then they will tend to gravitate back toward the ratio $(p_A/p_B)^*$. So

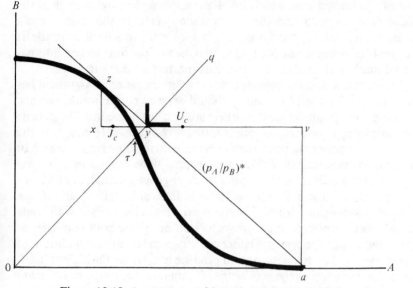

Figure 10.10. An outcome with trade surplus and deficit.

all the conclusions of section 10.2 carry over to the international economy: With economies of scale in production, the world economy may stabilize in a non-market-clearing configuration. In this case, the international economic system can be kept functioning only if countries are willing to run sustained surpluses or deficits on their balances of trade. Figure 10.10 shows what this would mean in terms of our diagrammatic approach.

There are, as before, two countries with identical preferences, endowments, and technologies. No market-clearing prices exist, but $(p_A/p_B)^*$ comes nearer to clearing the market than any other price ratio. One country, which we call U for United States, specializes in producing the constant-returns good, and the other, which we call J for Japan, produces mainly, though not exclusively, the increasing-returns good at z. Consumer demands are relatively intensive in the increasing-returns good; that is, the slope of the ray $0q$ is less than, but not far from, the slope of the line $0z$.

In this case, J wishes to export zx of B and import xy of A. U, however, wishes to export vy of A and import av of B. These trades are incompatible, as they would lead to a total worldwide consumption of $2y$, whereas world-wide total production is $(a + z)$, which is different from $2y$. Suppose now that U manages to import everything that it wants, but is unable to export enough to pay for it. Then it consumes at a point such as U_c

outside its budget line, which involves exporting less by value than the value of its imports and running a trade deficit. In this case, J must consume at a point J_c satisfying $J_c = (a + z) - U_c$, which will be inside its budget line. Being inside the budget line means spending less on international markets than is earned and thus running a trade surplus.

This example is in an important sense arbitrary, since no argument has been given about why U_c and J_c should arise as consumption vectors. However, the point is that if markets are to clear, there must be deficits and surpluses, giving rise to consumption levels such as U_c and J_c. In the long run, the pattern of trade surpluses and deficits shown in Figure 10.10 could only be sustained if there were capital flows from J to U, with J accumulating claims on the capital stock or government debt of U.

A point of interest in Figure 10.10 is that, although U_c and J_c are consumption vectors that allow the markets to clear, albeit with trade imbalances, these consumption vectors do not allow both countries to gain from trade. The best that either country could do under conditions of autarchy would be to consume and produce at τ, where the highest indifference curve touches the production frontier. As the diagram is drawn, country U is better off at U_c than at τ, but J is worse off at J_c than at τ.

Our next step is to put a little more structure on the kinds of consumption levels that could arise in such an international economy.

10.4   An institutional framework for managed trade

We have seen that if international trade is conducted within the framework of competitive markets, it may be impossible to achieve market clearing and trade balance: Situations can arise where markets clear only if sustained trade imbalances are allowed, with offsetting capital movements. It seems then very natural to enquire whether there is some alternative framework that will allow markets to clear and trade to balance and that will also allow all participants to enjoy gains from international trade.

Within the context of economic policy in a closed economy, it has long been recognized that the existence of substantial scale economies in production may require regulation rather than competition if efficiency and market clearing are to be achieved. This suggests that in the search for alternative institutional frameworks for conducting international trade, it is natural to consider an extension to the international economy of some of the regulatory frameworks already considered for a closed economy and discussed in Chapter 2. There are in fact many of these; we consider only one of them here, but any of them could in principle provide a logically coherent framework for the analysis of managed trade.

We analyze a particular regulatory framework where firms, instead of

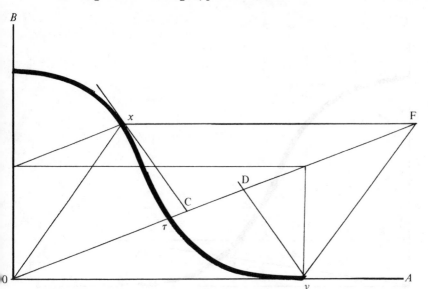
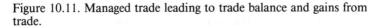

Figure 10.11. Managed trade leading to trade balance and gains from trade.

maximizing profits taking prices as given, sell at levels of outputs where prices are equal to marginal cost. This is a classical and widely studied approach to the regulation of economies-of-scale industries.[2] We look at its implications for international trade in order to illustrate the possibilities.

Figure 10.11 illustrates, within the now-familiar framework, the kind of equilibrium that can arise if instead of requiring firms to maximize profits, we require only that they price at marginal cost. In Figure 10.11, consumers are, as usual, maximizing utility subject to a budget constraint, and firms are producing where marginal cost is equal to price, or exceeds price if the output of a good is zero. In this case it is possible to show rigorously that, under very general conditions, there are prices at which markets clear and trade balances, in spite of the increasing returns.[3] Figure 10.11 illustrates such an outcome. Production occurs at x and y, and $F = x + y$ because yF is drawn parallel to $0x$. Countries consume at C and

[2] For related literature, see Nancy Ruggles, "Recent Developments in the Theory of Marginal Cost Pricing," *Review of Economic Studies* 17(1949–50), 107–26.
[3] See, for example, Donald Brown and Geoffrey Heal, "Marginal versus Average Cost Pricing in the Presence of a Natural Monopoly," *American Economic Review, Papers and Proceedings,* 73(2) (May 1983), 189–93. A still more general treatment can be found in Donald Brown, Geoffrey Heal, Ali Kahn, and Rajiv Vohra, "On a General Existence Theorem for Marginal Cost Pricing Equilibria," *Journal of Economic Theory* (in press).

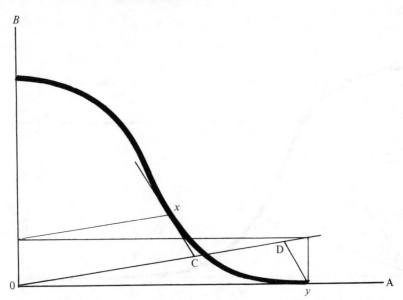

Figure 10.12. One country may lose from managed trade.

D, and a little elementary geometry confirms that C + D = F. Clearly both C and D are preferable to τ, the best that either country can achieve without trade. It follows that, at least for this example, we have combined the following three desiderata: (1) markets clearing, (2) trade balancing, and (3) both countries gaining from trade.

Unfortunately, it is not always possible to combine all three in this way. We can always find prices giving conditions 1 and 2 – market clearing and trade balance – but at these prices one country may lose from trade.

Figure 10.12 shows such a case: The country consuming at D is much better off than under autarchy, while its partner at C is much worse off than without trade. Since the losing country has no incentive to engage in trade, without further provisions it could be expected to drop out of the international economic system, of course depriving its trading partner of the possible gains from trade. In such a situation, the gaining country clearly has an incentive to persuade its potential partner to stay in the international market. It can be shown, at least within the very simple geometric framework used here, that the gainer gains more than the loser loses, so that the gainer could offer to transfer enough wealth to the loser to make the loser better off than under autarchy, and could still retain for itself a net gain from trade.

A related point is that, because both countries are assumed to be identical, there is no obvious way of deciding which would produce at x and which at y – a very important decision, given that the former will make a substantial welfare gain and the latter a welfare loss. If there were a pre-trade agreement among the countries to divide the gains from trade equally, or in some other other mutually agreeable fashion, then these problems would be resolved. This suggests that, under a system of managed trade, there would be international pretrade bargaining about the division of the gains from trade, and about which country is to be assigned to each pattern of production. A brief study of the history of customs unions certainly reveals many instances of this type; indeed, such negotiations are a regular feature of life in the European Economic Community.

Enough has now been said to show that there is at least one way in which one can begin to give content to the concept of managed trade, and to show that this may provide a manner of coordinating international transactions superior to competitive free trade. There are several other alternative approaches that are possible. We conclude by remarking that if increasing-returns firms sell their output at marginal cost in international markets, then, of course, they must do so also in domestic markets. The regulation applied to the international market must therefore be consistent with that applied to the domestic market, which carries the implication that domestic regulatory schemes would have to be harmonized between trading countries.

CHAPTER 11

North – South trade and export policies

We described in Chapter 4 the potential drawbacks of export-led policies based upon the exports of traditional commodities; we also described the conditions under which such policies can be expected to succeed. This chapter gives a geometric explanation of these results, based on a theory of trade and development that has been developed formally in a number of publications.[1] The purpose here is to provide an illustration of how, and under what conditions, the shortcomings of export-led policies arise, and also to show when it is desirable to increase exports.

Our first example is a country or region that exports a labor intensive commodity and has two characteristics: abundant labor and dual technologies.

11.1 Abundant labor: Heckscher – Ohlin and Lewis

Abundant labor is here a property of the supply function of labor. It means that labor supply responds positively and strongly to increases in the real wage. Formally, the labor supply function takes the form

$$L^S = \alpha(w/p_B) + \bar{L},$$

where L^S denotes supply of labor, $\bar{L}$ is a constant, w/p_B is the real wage (the wage w divided by the price of basics p_B), and α is a positive number. Abundant labor supply in this case means a large value for α; thus as the real wage w/p_B increases, labor supply L^S increases very sharply. We could

---

[1] See, for example, various works by G. Chichilnisky: "Terms of Trade and Domestic Distribution: Export-Led Growth with Abundant Labor," Discussion Paper no. 41, Harvard Institute for International Development, 1978; "Terms of Trade and Domestic Distribution: Export-Led Growth with Abundant Labor," *Journal of Development Economics,* 1(2) (April 1981), 163–92; "North–South Trade and Export-Led Policies," *Journal of Development Economics,* 15(1–3) (May–Aug. 1984), 131–60; "North–South Trade: A Rejoinder to Rejoinders," *Journal of Development Economics,* 15(1–3) (May–Aug. 1984), 177–84; (with S. Cole) "Expansion of the North and Exports of the South," Harvard Institute for International Development, 1978, revised January 1981; (with D. McLeod) "Agricultural Productivity and Trade: The Case of Argentina," Working Paper, World Bank, 1984; (with G. Heal and J. Podivinsky) "Trade between Sri Lanka and the U.K.: A Case Study in North–South Trade," Working Paper, Columbia University, Graduate School of Business, 1983.

Wages

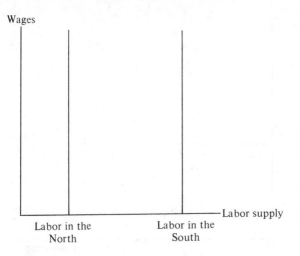

Labor in the
North

Labor in the
South

Labor supply

Figure 11.1. Heckscher–Ohlin's labor supply function: A constant.

also use other supply functions such as $L^S = (w/p_B)^\alpha$ and obtain similar results.

This notion of abundance of labor is different from that of the Heckscher–Ohlin model. The latter refers to a relatively large *fixed* pool of labor. In algebraic terms abundance in the Heckscher–Ohlin sense means that $L^S = L$, where L is a relatively large positive number.

Our definition, instead, measures abundance by the response of labor supply to real wages. In this sense it is closer to W. Arthur Lewis's concept of unlimited labor supply. Far from considering a large constant pool of labor, Lewis views very abundant labor in the South as an infinite sensitivity of labor supply to real wages: Labor is supplied in unlimited amounts at the subsistence wage. In effect, this pegs the real wage in his model at a *subsistence wage*.

Lewis's case represents a limiting case of our assumption of great responsiveness of labor supply to wages: Our response parameter α is infinite in his case. In our case, however, the response parameter α is large but finite, so that real wages vary with changes in supply; they are *not* pegged to the subsistence level.

The Heckscher–Ohlin case can also be viewed as a limiting case of our supply function for labor, the case when the parameter measuring labor response to wages is zero (i.e., $\alpha = 0$). Our model thus includes both Lewis's ($\alpha = \infty$) and that of Heckscher–Ohlin ($\alpha = 0$) as special cases.

Figures 11.1–11.3 portray these three assumptions about labor supply: Heckscher–Ohlin's, Lewis's, and our assumptions, respectively. Our

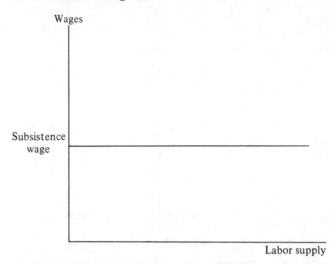

Figure 11.2. Arthur Lewis's labor supply function: infinitely elastic labor supply at the subsistence wage.

labor supply assumption is clearly intermediate to Heckscher–Ohlin's and Lewis's. We have more flexibility than either of those two models because we can adjust the parameter α to fit the economy under consideration. For instance, we generally take α in the North to be small, so that there, labor supply is close to constant; this is the Heckscher–Ohlin case. In the South, instead, α is large, so that its labor supply behavior is closer to the Lewis case. Empirical studies of labor supply conditions in Argentina, Mexico, Sri Lanka, the United Kingdom, and the United States, confirm these general assumptions.[2]

11.2   Dual technologies in the South, homogeneous technologies in the North

The second feature of the economy that is important in our analysis is the level of duality. The South's technology is assumed to be rather dual. By contrast, the technology in the North is assumed to be relatively homogeneous. These notions of *duality* and *homogeneity* in technologies are formalized in the following.

We suppose, as in the Heckscher–Ohlin model, that each region produces and consumes two goods. We call these basics, denoted by B, and industrial goods, denoted by I.

Our production functions take the form

---

[2] See the references in footnote 1.

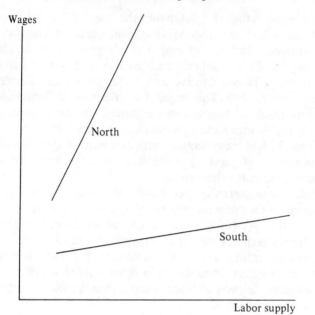

Wages

North

South

Labor supply

Figure 11.3. Labor supply in the Chichilnisky model: more responsive to real wages in the South than in the North.

$$B = \min \left(L^B/a_1, K^B/c_1 \right), \tag{11.1}$$

$$I = \min \left(L^I/a_2, K^I/c_2 \right), \tag{11.2}$$

that is, we have Leontieff-type technologies with fixed factor proportions. Here L^B and L^I are the inputs of labor into sectors B and I, respectively; K^B and K^I are the inputs of capital into the two sectors; a_1 and a_2 are labor-output coefficients, and c_1 and c_2 the capital-output coefficients, in B and I, respectively.

These production functions are used merely for simplicity of exposition. There is nothing intrinsic about them. One could equally well utilize Cobb–Douglas or constant elasticity of substitution (CES) production functions and obtain similar results, though at the cost of considerably more algebra.

Consider now the determinant D of the matrix

$$\begin{pmatrix} a_1 & a_2 \\ c_1 & c_2 \end{pmatrix}, \quad D = a_1 c_2 - a_2 c_1.$$

This number can be used to "measure" the degree of duality or homogeneity of this region's technology. When the two sectors use the same technology, we have the maximum degree of homogeneity possible; then

$a_1 = a_2$ and $c_1 = c_2$, so that $D = 0$. On the other hand if B is very labor-intensive and uses little capital, then a_1 is large and c_1 is small; likewise, if I is very capital-intensive and uses little labor, c_2 is large and a_2 small. Then D becomes a large positive number, which goes to infinity as the sector B becomes extremely labor-intensive and I extremely capital-intensive. Thus D measures duality: The larger it is, the more different are the proportions in which the two sectors use inputs, and the more dual the economy; when D is small, the economy is *homogeneous*.

In either case, with homogeneous or with dual technologies, D is always a positive number when good B is more labor-intensive than I. This is an assumption that we make throughout.

It is possible to interpret this concept of duality geometrically. Consider a given set of prices for this economy: p_B, p_I, w, and r. At these prices labor supply is fixed at $L' = \alpha(w/p_B) + \overline{L}$, and capital supply at $K' = \beta r + \overline{K}$.

The next step is to characterize geometrically the transformation (production possibility) frontier between the two outputs B and I. Recall that the production functions are as shown in equations (11.1) and (11.2). If the output levels of the two goods are B and I, then the total quantities of capital and labor used are

$$\text{capital used} = K^D = c_1 B + c_2 I,$$
$$\text{labor used} = L^D = a_1 B + a_2 I.$$

Since the outputs B and I must be within the productive capacity of the economy, it is clearly necessary that

$$K^D = c_1 B + c_2 I \leq K' \tag{11.3}$$

and

$$L^D = a_1 B + a_2 I \leq L'. \tag{11.4}$$

Consider now the equation

$$c_1 B + c_2 I = K'. \tag{11.5}$$

This describes the combinations of basic and industrial goods whose capital requirements exactly exhaust the available supply of capital. Equation (11.5) gives a relationship between B and I with a slope of $-c_2/c_1$. Similarly, the equation

$$a_1 B + a_2 I = L' \tag{11.6}$$

describes the output combinations of B and I that just use up the total labor supply L'. Equation (11.6) gives a relationship between B and I with a slope of $-a_2/a_1$.

In Figure 11.4, the lines (11.5) and (11.6) are shown. The difference in their slopes is

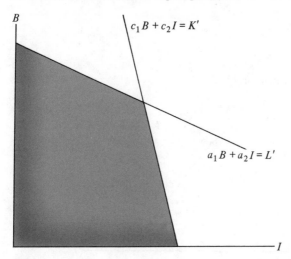

Figure 11.4. The production possibility set at p_B, p_I, w, and r.

$$-a_2/a_1 - (-c_2/c_1), \quad \text{which is} \quad (a_1c_2 - a_2c_1)/a_1c_1 = D/a_1c_1,$$

where D is the determinant of the matrix of input–output coefficients. When $D = 0$, the two lines are parallel; the bigger is D, the larger is the angle between them.

As the feasible outputs of B and I have to satisfy both (11.3) and (11.4), the frontier of the production possibility set is given by the set whose upper boundary is the lower envelope of the two lines in Figure 11.4: This area is shown shaded. Figure 11.5 shows this set when D is nearly zero, so that $(-c_2/c_1)$ and $(-a_2/a_1)$ are similar and D is small: The frontier is nearly a straight line. This corresponds to what we shall refer to as *homogeneous technologies*. Figure 11.6 portrays *dual technologies*: $(-c_2/c_1)$ and $(-a_2/a_1)$ are very different, so that D is large, and there is a sharp kink in the frontier.

Two further points should be made about the geometry of the production possibility set. Figures 11.4–11.6 all show that the line (11.6) denoting full use of labor, intersects the B-axis below the line (11.5), denoting full employment of capital. This follows naturally from the assumption that B is labor-intensive and that I is capital-intensive. Expanding production of the labor-intensive good, that is, moving up the B-axis, will naturally use up all labor before it uses up all capital, and vice versa.

A second point is that since labor and capital supplies L' and K', which are the right-hand sides of equations (11.5) and (11.6), respectively, are given by the equations

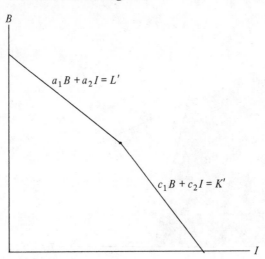

Figure 11.5. The production set with homogeneous technologies.

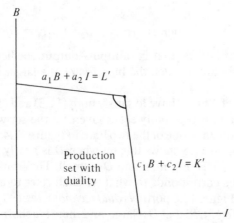

Figure 11.6. The production set with dual technologies.

$$L' = \alpha w/p_B + \overline{L},$$
$$K' = \beta r + \overline{K},$$

they depend on w, p_B, and r. Labor and capital supplies alter if these prices change. Therefore as prices change, the whole production frontier changes, as the lines (11.5) and (11.6) move in and out.

In particular, if labor is abundant, then α is large, and changes in the real wage w/p_B will lead to large movements in the line (11.6): A rise in

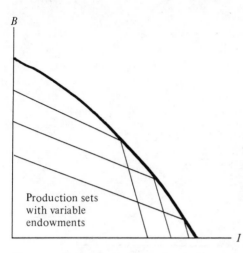

Figure 11.7. A production frontier with variable endowments.

w/p_B will shift this part of the boundary of the production possibility set sharply upward and vice versa. If $\alpha = \beta = 0$, so that $L' = \overline{L}$ and $K' = \overline{K}$, then the production frontier is fixed and does not vary with prices. Figure 11.7 depicts a variable-price production frontier, which is the outer envelope of the frontiers for all possible prices.

11.3   Increased exports and their prices

All the pieces are now in place for deriving geometrically the impact of an increase in exports on the exporting economy. First, let us visualize the relationship between domestic consumption and exports at a given set of prices.

Assume, as is usually the case, that both goods are produced in positive quantities. Production occurs at the point p, the intersection of the lines

$$c_1 B + c_2 I = K^D = K' = \beta r + \overline{K}$$

and

$$a_1 B + a_2 I = L^D = L' = \alpha w + \overline{L}.$$

Now, assume that the relative price of basics p_B/p_I goes up. This means a rotation of the price line p_B/p_I as indicated in Figure 11.8. At the new price $(p_B/p_I)'$, both the market-clearing real wages w/p_B and the rate of return on capital r, change. These relationships are given by the zero-profit conditions

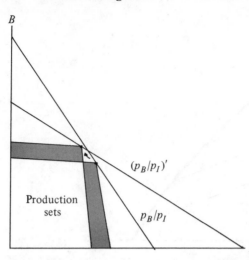

Figure 11.8. Change in the production possibility frontier due to a change in prices.

$$p_B = a_1 w + c_1 r, \tag{11.7}$$
$$p_I = a_2 w + c_2 r. \tag{11.8}$$

From now on we assume that $p_I = 1$, so that p_B now represents the relative price p_B/p_I of basic to industrial goods. An increase in p_B now means a drop in the relative price of I and an increase in that of B. When $p_I = 1$, we obtain from inverting the price equations (11.7) and (11.8)

$$w = \frac{a_2 p_B - a_1}{D} \tag{11.9}$$

and

$$r = \frac{c_1 - c_2 p_B}{D}. \tag{11.10}$$

These show that, when D is positive, wages w are an increasing function of the price of the labor-intensive good, p_B, and the rate of return on capital, r, a decreasing function of p_B. At a higher price p_B, real wages w/p_B increase, and the rate of return on capital r drops. Therefore capital supply decreases and labor supply increases, since $K^S = \beta r + \bar{K}$ and $L^S = \alpha w/p_B + \bar{L}$. The production possibility frontier thus shifts as shown in Figure 11.8. In Figure 11.8, the price line $(p_B/p_I)'$ is flatter because the relative price of B has increased. For the same reason, the total supply of B

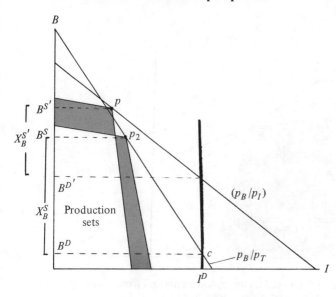

Figure 11.9. A decrease in exports as the price of basics p_B rises.

has increased and that of I has decreased: A higher p_B means more labor in total and less capital in total, and good B is labor-intensive.

We can now explore the impact of an expansion in exports of B, which is denoted X_B^S. In Figure 11.9, I^D denotes domestic demand for industrial goods, and at prices p_B/p_I, the country consumes at c, exporting $X_B^S = B^S - B^D$ and importing $X_I^D = I^D - I^S$.

Figure 11.9 shows that exports of basics decrease from X_B^S to $X_B^{S'}$ when the relative price of basics p_B increases. This is due to the change in prices, as industrial demand I^D is held constant.

Now consider the case where industrial demand I^D increases as a response to the relatively lower price of industrial goods (i.e., a higher p_B). It is clear from Figure 11.9 that the drop in exports X_B^S could still occur, even though it would be less pronounced.

The drop in exports of B as p_B rises is not due to a drop in the domestic output of B; in Figures 11.8 and 11.9, the output of B has actually increased. The reason is that when p_B increases, real wages and employment also increase. The domestic demand for B then increases so rapidly that, even at the higher level of output, less is available for exports. Under these circumstances, the only way exports can be increased is for there to be a drop in the relative price of basics. This also means a drop in real wages, employment, and domestic output, by (11.9) and the labor supply equation.

Consider now such a drop in p_B. The economy moves from the output

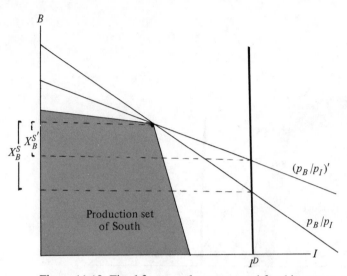

Figure 11.10. Fixed factor endowments and fixed investment demand: As exports expand, their prices drop.

level p to the output level p^2: It produces less basics, but it consumes domestically proportionately less than before. Exports thus increase as their price p_B drops. By (11.9) real wages also drop when exports decrease.

Figures 11.8 and 11.9 provide not a proof but an illustration of the results. They actually show the effects of duality and the abundance of labor on the production set: These make the production possibility set more "square," and shift the upper boundary of this set upward as p_B/p_I increases. Under such conditions, an increase in exports tends to be associated with lower output, as well as with a lower price for and domestic consumption of basics.

It is also possible to derive these results for economies where labor is not abundant, provided that one makes certain assumptions about the pattern of demand. This issue is considered next.

11.4   Fixed factor endowments: a geometric proof

Suppose that the production set remains constant as prices change, as would be the case with factor endowments that are fixed. Then it is always the case that, if industrial demand remains constant, exports X_B^S only increase when their price drops. Figure 11.10 illustrates this case.

If industrial demand, rather than being a constant, increases with capital income rK, then as p_B/p_I increases, industrial demand will drop. This

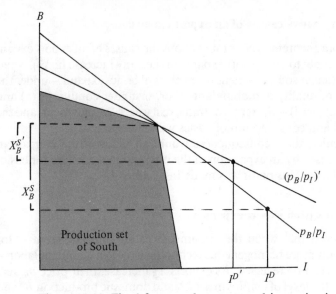

Figure 11.11. Fixed factor endowments and increasing industrial demand: As exports expand, their prices drop.

in turn implies, as shown in Figure 11.11, that domestic demand for basics rises and exports X_B^S always drop as p_B/p_I increases. So in both of these cases, the South's terms of trade *must* drop if it is to increase the level of its exports.

Figures 11.10 and 11.11 illustrate the following cases:

(a) Factor supplies are fixed, $L = L$ and $K = \overline{K}$, and either
(b) Industrial demand is fixed, $I^D = \overline{I}^D$, or
(c) Industrial demand rises with capital income rK.

Note that (c) is always true when wage income wL is spent entirely on the basic good. In this case the national income identity $p_B B^D + p_I I^D = wL + rK$ implies that capital income is spent on I, so that (c) holds. So we could replace (c) by its equivalent:

(d) Wage income wL is spent on the export good.

Figures 11.10 and 11.11 provide a complete proof of the following theorem: "Suppose condition (a) and any one of conditions (b), (c), or (d) hold. Then exports X_B^S can only increase when the terms of trade p_B, real wages w/p_B, employment of labor L, and domestic production B^S and consumption B^D of B all decrease."

11.5   Alternative causes of an export expansion

Note that our theorems say nothing about the causes of an export expansion. They apply to any export expansion (i.e., any increase in X_B^S), whatever its particular source. Whenever exports of basics expand – under the conditions of duality and abundant labor, or under conditions (a) and either (b), (c), or (d) – the terms of trade, real wages, employment, and the production and consumption of basics will all decline.

In particular, these consequences would all follow if the increase in exports is caused by an expansion of the international demand for basics from the North. This point was made in Chapter 4.

11.6   Gains from export expansion

It is of interest that when the circumstances are quite different – for example, with more homogeneous technologies or less abundant labor – these results can be reversed. As exports X_B^S increase, their price p_B, real wages w/p_B, the level of employment L^S, and domestic production B^S and domestic consumption B^D of basics all increase in the South.

11.7   An expansion of industrial demand in the North

We have so far studied the effects of a change in the North's demand for basics. Our final task is to study the impact of an expansion of demand for industrial goods in the North, $I^D(N)$. Figure 11.12 illustrates the impact of an increase in the level of $I^D(N)$. Recall that in the North technologies are homogeneous and capital is abundant.

When equilibrium consumption of industrial goods $I^D(N)$ in the North rises, and that in the South $I^D(S)$ remains constant, then we must move to a new equilibrium at which the total worldwide consumption of industrial goods is higher. This means that the new equilibrium must be characterized by a higher supply of industrial goods; under the model's assumptions about factor supplies and factor intensities, however, a higher supply will only be forthcoming at a higher relative price p_I/p_B. So a rise in $I^D(N)$ must lead to a rise in p_I/p_B, and the South's terms of trade, p_B/p_I, will therefore drop. The supply of industrial goods rises in the North. The North also imports more basics at a lower price, and in fact consumes more of both basic and industrial goods at the new equilibrium.

Because the South has dual technologies and abundant labor, the drop in the terms of trade p_B/p_I is associated with a rise in exports X_B^S and with lower real wages, employment, and domestic consumption of basics in the South. A dismal story for the South, but a happy one for the North:

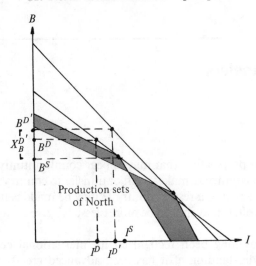

Figure 11.12. An expansion of the industrial country's demand for basics is associated with a drop in their price.

Through an increase in the South's exports initiated by an expansion of the North's demand, there is a transfer of welfare away from the South and toward the North.

Note that if, instead, the South had homogeneous technologies and more abundant capital, an industrial expansion in the North would still lead to lower terms of trade for the South (p_B/p_I must drop), but this time it would also lead to *lower exports* from the South. Thus in this case the North does not increase its consumption of both goods I and B; instead it shifts its consumption away from basics and toward industrial goods. This also happens in the South.

CHAPTER 12

Aid and transfers

12.1 Introduction

Chapter 6 made use of a proposition that may appear counterintuitive. The proposition is that if country H makes a gift or transfer to country L, then it is entirely possible that as a result country H may be made better off, and country L worse off. It may indeed be more blessed to give than to receive.

This phenomenon has long been recognized in international economics, though our understanding of it has been advanced greatly in recent years. Because the basic result is surprising, and because it is important for understanding the complications associated with aid and loans, we present below a simple geometric explanation. First, however, we provide an intuitive discussion of the underlying economics.[1]

The point is actually very simple and hinges on the relative magnitudes of income and substitution effects, and on the response of market prices to a policy change. Suppose H to make a gift to L. Obviously, if prices stay constant, H is poorer and L is richer, so H can consume less and L more: H loses and L gains.

Now suppose in addition that L consumes very intensively good A, so that most of L's extra wealth is spent on good A. Obviously, we expect the price of A to rise as a result of the transfer: Wealth has been redistributed toward consumers with a strong demand for A. Finally, assume that country H, the donor country, is the main supplier of good A. Then H will benefit from the price increase caused by its gift, and indeed it is perfectly possible that this benefit outweighs the loss from the original gift. Hence the paradoxical conclusion that the donor may gain, and so the recipient lose, from a gift.

It is not difficult to think of examples that seem to meet the conditions

[1] The analysis in this chapter draws from: G. Chichilnisky, "Basic Goods, Commodity Transfers and the International Economic Order," *Journal of Development Economics* 7(4) (1980) 505–19; J. Geanakoplos and G. M. Heal, "A Geometric Explanation of the Transfer Paradox in a Stable Economy," *Journal of Development Economics*, 13(1–2) (1983), 223–36; G. Chichilnisky, "The Transfer Problem with Three Agents Once Again: Characterization, Uniqueness and Stability," *Journal of Development Economics* 13(1–2) (1983), 237–48; and G. Chichilnisky and G. M. Heal, "To Give or to Destroy," Working Paper, Columbia University, 1984.

indicated above. The United States exports food and armaments. Many countries receiving U.S. aid have high propensities to import both. So it is possible that aid given by the United States will increase demand for its exports sufficiently to raise their prices. A big enough price movement could leave the United States better off. Similarly, if OPEC gives aid to countries with a high propensity to import oil, then this could be reflected in a firmer price for oil.

These effects can clearly be substantial: In Chapter 6, we noted the effect of loans to Central and South America on demand for U.S. exports. In fact, the problem may arise in a more acute form. If aid is used by the recipient country to develop an export sector, then it may lead both to an increase in demand for the donor's exports, raising their prices, and to an increase in supply of the donor's imports (the recipient's exports), lowering their prices. Both mechanisms will improve the donor's terms of trade.

12.2 A formal model

Economists have known since the work of Leontief in 1936 that the "transfer paradox" is a logical possibility, but until recently it had always been considered a rare curiosity rather than something that had a significant chance of occurring. The reason for this is that Mundell showed that, in a world with two countries and two goods, it would only occur at a competitive equilibrium that was unstable in the Walrasian sense. In a two-good model without production, the framework within which these issues have usually been studied, Walrasian instability means that the excess demand for a good rises as its price rises, a somewhat counterintuitive property.[2] Recently, however, Chichilnisky demonstrated that if one relaxes the assumption of only two countries, then the "transfer paradox" can indeed occur at a competitive equilibrium that is Walrasian-stable.[3] In the following we give a diagrammatic presentation of this result for the case of three countries and two goods.

Call the goods A and B, and the countries H, M, and L, for high, medium and low – think of these as their income levels. Each country consumes goods A and B in fixed proportions: Their preferences are shown in Figure 12.1.

H consumes B intensively, L consumes A intensively, and M is in between. So we could think of B as a good that rich countries have a high

---

[2] In many-good models, the implications of Walrasian instability seem less unattractive. In fact, Walrasian instability can easily occur in such cases if there are several goods that are complements.

[3] See references in footnote 1.

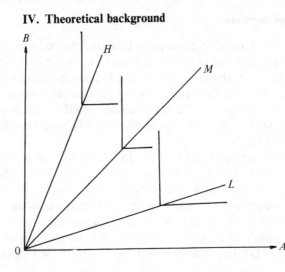

Figure 12.1 Preferences of countries H, M, and L.

propensity to consume (consumer electronics, for example), and A as a good that poorer countries have a high propensity to consume (food-stuffs). From now on, we shall just represent the preferences of these countries by their expansion paths, the rays $0H$, $0M$, and $0L$. Note that whatever their endowments, and whatever the market prices, H will always consume on the ray $0H$, M on the ray $0M$, and L on the ray $0L$.

Figure 12.2 demonstrates how the transfer paradox can occur at a stable equilibrium. The three countries initially have endowments at e_H, e_M, and e_L. Competitive equilibrium relative prices before the transfer are given by the slope of the lines (e_H, c_H), (e_M, c_M), and (e_L, c_L). These lines therefore constitute the budget lines of the countries, which consume respectively at c_H, c_M, and c_L. Country H exports A and imports B; M exports A and imports B; and L exports B and imports A. Because markets clear, the vector sum of the lines (e_H, c_H), (e_M, c_M), and (e_L, c_L), the net trades of the countries, must be zero.

Suppose now that country H reduces its endowment from e_H to e'_H by giving part of it to L, whose endowment therefore increases from e_L to e'_L. Country M's endowment stays constant at e_M.

This change in endowments leads to changes in amounts traded by the various countries, and so to new equilibrium prices. We have to work out what these are. To do this, draw the line (e'_L, c_L). The slope of this line represents a set of relative prices with the following property. If country L with new posttransfer endowment e'_L faced these prices, it would consume at c_L, exactly where it consumed before the transfer. So if the new equilibrium prices just happened to be given by the slope of (e'_L, c_L), country L would neither gain nor lose from the transfer. Clearly if the new budget

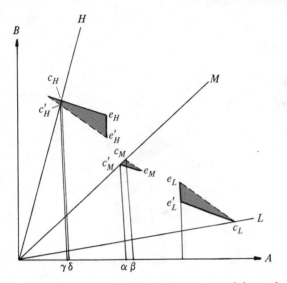

Figure 12.2. A transfer may harm the recipient when it imports the donor's export.

line were more nearly vertical than (e'_L, c_L), country L would lose: If it were more nearly horizontal than (e'_L, c_L), it would gain. The next step is to decide which of these cases will occur.

To do this, we consider what the demand for and supply of A would be at a price ratio given by the slope of (e'_L, c_L). The lines (e_M, c'_M) and (e'_H, c'_H) are parallel to (e'_L, c_L), so at these prices H, M, and L consume respectively at c'_H, c'_M, and c_L. Country H's demand for A has fallen by the amount $\gamma\delta$. Country M's demand for A has risen by $\alpha\beta$, and country L's is unchanged. Because $\alpha\beta$ is bigger than $\gamma\delta$ (this can be proven formally by elementary geometry), demand for A worldwide has increased; but the supply of goods is constant (total endowments are constant) and, as at the original prices demand equaled supply, there must now be an excess demand for A.

If the market is Walrasian-stable, an excess demand for A means that its price will rise: Hence the final budget line, after the transfer, will be steeper than (e'_L, c_L). The recipient country L will be worse off after the transfer than before, and this has occurred in a stable market.

It still remains to be shown that the donor country H gains from the transfer. It would be tedious to go through this argument too. Note, however, that at c'_H, H is nearly as well off as before the transfer and, if the price of A rises so that the budget line becomes nearer vetical, it is clearly possible that H will end up consuming more than at c_H, and so gaining.

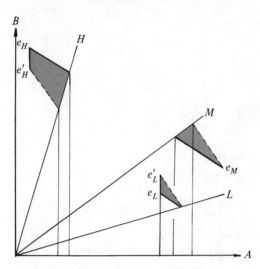

Figure 12.3. The recipient may gain if it and the donor export the same good.

One can give a formal argument to this effect.[4] In the end, then, the recipient L loses from the transfer, and both other countries – donor H and nonparticipant M – gain.

Figure 12.3 shows a different configuration, in which H is an exporter, rather than importer, of the good that it consumes intensively. Exactly the same geometric construction as before can be used to show that in this case both donor and recipient are made worse off by the transfer; however, the nonparticipant gains.

One final point should be noted about these results: The denomination of the transfer is immaterial. The diagrams show this as involving a mixture of both goods, and all of the above arguments hold for a transfer involving the goods in any proportions. If one of them is thought of as a numeraire, then the transfer could be entirely in units of the numeraire.

12.3   Supply responses

It was mentioned in Chapter 6 that the possible negative effects of a transfer on its recipient could be offset by a suitable increase in domestic output. In Figure 12.4, we indicate the intuitive basis for this claim: A

---

[4] See Geanakoplos and Heal (op. cit.).

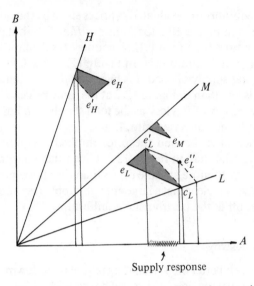

Figure 12.4. A supply response reduces the negative impact of a transfer.

fully rigorous analysis would require the explicit modeling of the production side of the economy, something that cannot be done geometrically.[5]

Figure 12.4 deals with the same case as Figure 12.2, with the following further development. When the price of good A rises relative to that of good B, the country L has the opportunity to convert some of its endowment of good B into extra good A. One can think of this conversion as an aggregative way of modeling a supply response to an increase in the price of A relative to B: If A and B were both produced goods, then such a price change would lead to an alteration of the output mix in favor of A.

In Figure 12.4, when the price of A changes from the slope of (e_L, c_L) to the slope of (e'_L, c_L), country L's endowment moves from e'_L to e''_L. B is converted into A at a rate of transformation given by the slope of (e'_L, e''_L): This rate is determined by the underlying production possibilities.

It is clear from the diagram that the presence of this supply response will make country L better off than it would be in its absence, provided that the line (e'_L, e''_L) is less steep than the line (e'_L, c_L), that is, provided that the rate of transformation in production is more favorable to L than is the price ratio given by the slope of (e'_L, e_L).

In the case shown in Figure 12.4, the changes in demand for good A

[5] There is a mathematical analysis of this case in G. Chichilnisky, G. M. Heal, and D. L. McLeod, "Resources, Trade and Debt," Discussion Paper, Division of Global Analysis and Projections, World Bank, 1984.

relative to the intitial equilibrium, evaluated at prices given by the slope of (e'_L, c_L), are the same as in Figure 12.2 for countries H and M, but are of course different for country L. In Figure 12.2, country L's demand for A was the same as at the initial equilibrium: In Figure 12.4, this demand is bigger by α, but the total supply of good A is bigger by $\beta > \alpha$. Hence the excess demand for A is less than in Figure 12.2 at the same prices. Correspondingly, the excess supply of B is less, as the total supply of B has been reduced by some of it being converted into A.

The rise in the price of A, beyond the price implied by (e'_L, c_L), is therefore less in Figure 12.4 than in Figure 12.2. Given that country L's endowment e''_L is also worth more at these prices than the endowment e'_L with no supply response, it is clear that a large enough supply response can ensure that L is better off at the posttransfer equilibrium.

12.4   To give or to destroy

A country may make itself better off by donating part of its endowment to another. In fact, a more striking proposition can be established: If country H can raise its consumption levels by donating endowment to another country, it can raise its consumption even more by destroying – throwing away – part of its endowment. One proves this by arguments very similar to those used in Figures 12.2 and 12.3. At some intuitive level, this point has long been recognized in the agricultural sector, where the destruction of produce in years of abundant crops has often been used as a way of supporting prices and raising farmers' incomes.